25 Role Plays
for
Negotiation Skills

**Ira Asherman and
Sandy Asherman**

**Human Resource Development Press, Inc.
Amherst, Massachusetts**

Published by HRD Press
22 Amherst Road
Amherst, MA 01002
1-800-822-2801

ISBN 0-87425-997-5

Production services by Clark Riley

Cover design by Old Mill Graphics

Editorial services by Lisa Wood

Contents

Role Plays	Page #	INDUSTRY Retail	Pharmaceutical	Supermarket	Manufacturing	Publishing	General	TOPIC Sales	Purchasing	Employee Performance	Boundary Roles	Angry Coworkers	General Management
1. The New Bicycle	5						✓	✓					✓
2. The Alpha Project	11	✓											✓
3. The Angry Customer	17						✓	✓				✓	
4. The Garage Sale	23						✓	✓					✓
5. The Work Request	29						✓						
6. Purchasing Problem	35								✓				
7. The Boundary Role	43		✓								✓		
8. The Purchasing Role	49				✓				✓		✓		
9. Consultant	55		✓										✓
10. The Guest Speaker	61						✓	✓					✓
11. Damaged Goods	69	✓					✓	✓					
12. The Antique Car	75	✓						✓					
13. The Stereo System	81												
14. The Safety Reports	87				✓								✓
15. The Salary Increase	93						✓					✓	
16. The Medical Conference	101		✓				✓						✓
17. The Job Posting	107						✓						
18. The Vacation "Buy"	113					✓	✓						✓
19. Late Again	119						✓						
20. The Outburst	125				✓		✓			✓			✓
21. The Poor Performance	131				✓					✓		✓	
22. The District Manager	137						✓			✓			✓
23. The Software System	143						✓			✓			✓
24. Supermarket Buyer	149			✓									✓
25. The HABA Buyer	155			✓				✓					

Introduction

This book of practice negotiations has been designed for the Management Training and Development Specialist who needs one or two role plays (practice negotiations), either to fit into an already existing program or for the design of a new negotiation program.

Most of the practice negotiations in this book were originally designed for use in *The Successful Negotiator*, a program we have conducted for a variety of clients. Others were developed by other management development professionals for use in negotiation or negotiation-related programs. All have been used in one or more programs.

Our Approach

These practice negotiations were designed to teach the Successful Negotiator approach to negotiation, which is a very specific one. The approach incorporates four critical concepts. They are:

- The understanding that successful negotiation is NOT an adversarial process, but one which establishes a collaborative framework for creative problem solving.
- The recognition that the needs and interests of both negotiating parties must be addressed if there is to be a long term solution.
- The understanding that negotiation is an ongoing process, and that today's negotiation will affect the long term relationship between the parties.
- The breakdown of the negotiating process into six distinct steps:

    1) Planning
    2) Climate Setting
    3) Issue Identification
    4) Bargaining
    5) Settlement
    6) Review

These six steps form the major units of *The Successful Negotiator* program, and the practice negotiations in this book are designed to illustrate the various steps in the process. In more detail, these steps are:

1

1) **Planning**

People often plan for a negotiation minutes before it is to take place. This unit stresses the importance of planning, and discusses in detail the factors to consider when preparing for a negotiation.

2) **Climate Setting**

The first few minutes of the negotiation set the stage for what is to follow — will the proceedings be formal, collaborative, business-like, or antagonistic? This unit places the control over the tone of the meeting in the hands of the negotiator and discusses the steps to take in establishing an appropriate climate.

3) **Issue Identification**

All too frequently negotiators move from a few words of greeting at the beginning of the negotiation to hammering out the details of the agreement, without outlining the issues to be negotiated. This unit teaches participants how to be clear, both about the objectives and the issues being negotiated.

4) **Bargaining**

In this unit the major negotiating strategies and tactics are reviewed, and each is discussed in a format that encourages an open, problem solving atmosphere. In this section one will gain a firm understanding of the different rituals involved in negotiation, their implications and how they can be most effectively used.

5) **Settlement**

After agreement is reached, what then? Many deals fall apart because this last step is not completed. This step summarizes the deal and ensures that both parties meet their obligations.

6) **Review**

This step is designed to aid the negotiator in assessing how well he/she conducted the negotiation and the degree to which he/she practiced the skills of the Successful Negotiator.

The practice negotiations in this book provide practice in Steps Two through Five. However, when you give participants time to plan and debrief, you are, in effect, practicing the entire six step process.

In addition to the six steps, there are also behaviors used most frequently by successful negotiators. We refer to these as the *critical behaviors*; they are described in the Resource Section of this manual.

The practice negotiations in this book cover a variety of fields. They are:

- *Sales* – Negotiations that focus on dealing with difficult customers, internal negotiations, and addressing customer needs.
- *Purchasing* – These negotiations look at the relationships between the purchasing staff and their internal clients.
- *Boundary Roles* – These focus on individuals who play boundary roles in their organization.

- *General Management* – These cover situations among coworkers, their mutual roles and their responsibilities to each other.
- *Employee Performance* – These negotiations provide practice in how to talk with one's employees about their performance.

The negotiations come from a variety of corporate settings. They are:

- Supermarkets
- Pharmaceutical Firms
- Retail Buying
- Medical Equipment Companies
- Publishing

There is a cover sheet for each negotiation which provides pertinent information about the role play, i.e., the time necessary, the objectives, and any special issues the trainer should be aware of in conducting the practice negotiation. Special issues are highlighted in the *Trainer Note*. The *Time Section* reflects the time needed to conduct the negotiation; it does not reflect the time needed for planning or debriefing. This is a decision you should make within the context of your program and its objectives. The *Objectives Section* provides the objectives the negotiation is designed to address.

Most of the practice negotiations are straightforward, although certain of them require special treatment if they are to work. That information is provided in the section called *Debriefing Note*.

You will also notice that we do not spend much time discussing the content of the negotiations. In our debriefings the primary concern is whether the participants practiced the specific skills and behaviors of the Successful Negotiator. However, certain of the role plays were designed both to look at the Six Step Model, and to raise specific content issues. We have usually indicated these in the objectives. Depending on your objectives, you might wish to discuss the content in greater detail. We have indicated where we believe it should be done.

Good luck.

Title:	**THE NEW BICYCLE** **#1**
Time:	Twenty Minutes
Objectives:	To illustrate: • the importance of trust in effective negotiating • creative problem solving
Trainer Note:	This practice negotiation is repeated twice, the first time as it is written. After completing it the first time, the group is told to complete the practice negotiation a second time, with the other person as their next door neighbor whom they like a great deal.
Debriefing Note:	After completing the initial negotiation (allow three or four minutes), ask what happened. Were they near a solution or were they arguing with the other person? Most of the groups will be arguing, with very little attempt at problem solving. Ask why this was the case. The usual answer will be, "I didn't know the other person. I was concerned with my needs, not theirs." In the initial negotiation, people tend to focus on themselves and their own needs.
After the Discussion:	Ask the group to conduct the negotiation a second time. However, this time, tell the group that the other person is their next door neighbor whom they like a great deal.
At the Conclusion:	Ask the group if the second time was any different and why. Most of the groups will indicate that it was much easier the second time because they knew each other and had a relationship. They cared about the other person. Compare the two experiences. You want the group to realize that the only variable was the relationship. The facts did not change, yet the outcomes were very different.
Closing:	Conduct a brief lecture on the importance of trust and relationships to effective negotiating. An excellent article is one by Dale Zand called "Trust and Managerial Problem Solving" from the Vol. 13, No. 2, 1972 issue of the *Administrative Science Quarterly*. Other articles can be found in *The Negotiation Sourcebook*, Asherman and Asherman, also published by HRD Press.

THE NEW BICYCLE
Person A

You have a serious problem. You promised your daughter a new bike for her birthday, but because of your extensive travel schedule, you couldn't even look for the bike until today (Friday). Her birthday is tomorrow and the party is tomorrow at noon. You're feeling guilty because you haven't been able to spend much time with her lately. In fact, you promised her not only the bike, but to go riding with her on the weekend. You can't disappoint her.

You called several stores and finally found one which has the bike in the exact size and color she wants. For your kid, it must be a very specific bike or it just won't do. You asked if they would hold the bike for you until you could get there — you even offered to give them your credit card number. The person you spoke with said, "Don't worry, no one else is going to buy it — just get down here."

As you walked down the aisle where the bikes are located, you see that another person is heading for "your" bike and calling a salesperson to help. You both reach the bike at the same time and quickly realize there is only one there. It has a sticker on it which says "last one."

THE NEW BICYCLE
Person B

Today is Friday and you have a serious problem. Your daughter's bike was stolen earlier in the week and she's entered in a bicycle race tomorrow at noon. She is the defending champion in the girl's division. When the bike was stolen, you promised her that you would get a new one, but because of working late every night, you haven't even had a chance to look for it until a few hours ago. This is the third store you've gone to and it's the only one that has the bike. You spoke with your spouse earlier and he/she let you know that your daughter was expecting the bike and had already told all her friends she was getting one. To quote your spouse, "we can't disappoint her."

As you walk down the aisle, you see another person heading for the same bike. You both reach the bike at the same time and quickly realize that there is only one there. It has a sticker on it which says "last one."

Title:	**THE ALPHA PROJECT**	**#2**

Time:	*Ten Minutes* if used for Issue Identification.
	Thirty Minutes if used as a complete negotiation.
Objectives:	To illustrate the importance of Issue Identification.
	To highlight the skills required for successfully completing Issue Identification.
Trainer Note:	Although this role play can be used for an entire negotiation, we have used it very successfully in a narrower way, i.e., Issue Identification. If used for Issue Identification, it is helpful to model or *discuss the critical behaviors before the negotiation is conducted* and direct the observers to look for those behaviors.
Debriefing Note:	When using this negotiation for Issue Identification, ask participants to stop negotiating once all the issues are on the table. In debriefing this role play, you will find that many people move directly into Problem Solving without identifying all the issues. You should point this out. Ask what made identifying the issues so difficult. People usually report that they are trained to solve problems and as a result move to problem solving behaviors right away. Discuss the impact of moving to problem solving so quickly. What is the potential impact on the quality of the solution?
	For those who completed Issue Identification successfully, highlight what they did well. Ask what behaviors they used.
Conclusion:	If you have conducted programs in effective problem solving, point out the similarity in the processes. Namely, that one needs to understand the nature of the problem before rushing to find an answer.
	You also want to point out that clarifying issues provides the negotiation with an anchor. This becomes particularly helpful when people begin to wander from the issue; you can then refocus them.

THE ALPHA PROJECT
Jim

You and Chris have been working on the Alpha Project team for the past 18 months. You represent Information Services.

You and Chris are at the same organizational level; she was asked to chair the project team. While you like Chris and have enjoyed working with her in the past, you think her appointment was a mistake. A number of people, yourself included, would have been better choices. This project involves the implementation of a new software program that could have a significant impact on the company.

You are not happy with the way Chris has treated you on this project. Namely:

- She has made several major changes in your section of the Quarterly Report without asking for or getting your approval. You were away on a trip, but she could have gotten to you with a little effort.
- Chris has been meeting informally with other members of the team and, for some reason, never invites you.
- Chris has embarrassed you at several meetings by asking you to respond to questions you were not prepared to discuss.

You've also heard from others that Chris feels you were responsible for the team being late with its monthly reports. She never even talked about this with you!

Chris has asked to meet with you — probably because you missed the last meeting due to a client visit. In addition, you had your secretary call to say you may have to miss next week's meeting because of another trip. In the past six months you have missed three meetings and since you were recently assigned to a second project team, you will most likely miss others. In fact, because you are short staffed, you haven't even sent people to cover for you. It's been tough lately because several people retired and have not been replaced. As a result, your boss has gotten you involved in several other projects. As he said to you recently, "We need you to represent us on at least two other teams. Do what you have to to keep on top of the Alpha Project, but don't let these other projects slip." When you mentioned the importance of the Alpha Project, he indicated that he thought its potential was being overrated and said, "... anyway, we have no choice. We'll just have to do the best we can."

This is not an easy problem. Chris behaves as if Information Services has nothing to do but work on this project. Your department is short-staffed. This whole thing really bothers you. You don't want this project or Chris to fail, but you don't see any real options. You are glad Chris asked to meet, since you've wanted to get these issues settled for some time.

Known to Both Parties

Chris chairs the Alpha project team. Jim represents Information Services. Both are at the same organizational level.

THE ALPHA PROJECT
Chris

You were very excited when your boss asked you to chair the Alpha Project team 18 months ago. You never chaired a team before and feel that this could have a positive impact on your career. The project involves the implementation of a new software system which could have real value to the company. Jim is one of the team members and you have worked with him on other projects during the past several years. You generally find him responsive and easy to work with. However, he missed last month's meeting and just this morning called your secretary to say that he won't be available for next week's meeting. This is not typical. You're not happy with Jim's level of participation; you feel that he is ignoring his responsibilities to the team. Namely:

- Jim has missed three meetings already. All in the last six months (and he hasn't sent anyone as a replacement). Prior to that time he was at every meeting.
- Jim's unavailability for meetings has resulted in the team being late with its monthly status reports on two separate occasions.
- Several weeks ago you had to make major revisions in Jim's section of the Quarterly Report because what he turned in was inadequate. If he had submitted a draft to you like everyone else, the problem could have easily been solved. This is not typical of Jim.
- Several times in the past three months you called ad-hoc meetings and weren't able to reach Jim. It would have been helpful if he'd been available, since these were issues he was knowledgeable about.

You can't afford to let Jim sacrifice your reputation. His poor performance is affecting the team. What makes the problem worse is that several team members have commented to you about Jim's performance and the effect it is having on the team. As one member said, "We need Information Service's input. If Jim can't participate, then we need to get someone who can."

You have spoken with your boss about the problem. She agreed with you as to its importance, but suggested that you try to work it out with Jim before she gets involved.

You really don't want your boss to intervene since it would indicate that you can't handle tough problems. She did make it very clear that she is concerned and wants you to get the problem resolved — how is up to you. Both of you see this project as critical.

You have asked to meet with Jim in an effort to let him know how you feel and to see if these problems can be solved and put behind you. You have not talked to Jim about your concerns before today.

Known to Both Parties

Chris chairs the Alpha project team. Jim represents Information Services. Both are at the same organizational level.

Title:	**THE ANGRY CUSTOMER**	**#3**

Time:	*Fifteen Minutes* if used for identifying issues.
	Thirty Minutes as a complete negotiation.
Objective:	To illustrate Issue Identification in the sales process.
Trainer Note:	This negotiation is most effective in illustrating Issue Identification. It requires the sales rep to be effective in asking and answering questions and in demonstrating empathy.
	When used as a full negotiation, it is important to tell the sales rep that he/she has complete authority to make this deal.
Debriefing Note – Issue Identification:	Your primary focus should be on the behaviors involved in Issue Identification and with the avoidance of beginning Problem Solving too soon. The temptation to solve the problem is great. As with Negotiation #2, explore the advantages of not quickly going into Problem Solving. Typically what people realize is that they now have a better understanding of the other party's problem.
Complete Role Play:	In addition to issue identification and effective problem solving behaviors, also look at the different solutions that were identified and what allowed them to take place.
	The key to this role play is in the questioning technique of the sales rep, in surfacing the client's problem, being empathetic, and not fixing blame. It is also important that they not stress Marketing's anger. Unless this anger is expressed very carefully, it can easily upset the client.

JOE KIRK
Purchasing Agent

You have been the Purchasing Agent at Staunton Stationery for the past several years. During that time you have used many different products of many different companies — including those of ABC, a major printer of forms and general paper supplies.

Because of some bookkeeping mistake, the state-wide buying group you occasionally deal with gave you the group price, which is $6.85 per hundred for the B-1 Forms. You've been getting this price for the past two years. After some checking with one of your associates, you realized that this price was inappropriate. However, it was an honest mistake; you weren't looking to get a free ride. You'd really like to keep the lower price since it's contributed significantly to your bottom line this past year. Moreover, you have utilized these figures in your current year's fiscal budget, which still has three months to go. You also based your next year's figures on a small increase over $6.85, not the $15.25 quoted!

When Lee Stone, the ABC sales representative, quoted you that price over the phone, you just about hit the ceiling. That's a huge increase from the buying group cost, even though $15.25 is similar to ABC's competitor's (Glibb) price. There isn't much difference between the Glibb and ABC products, but your people clearly prefer ABC and the B-1 forms sell real well — your customers like them.

What really makes you mad is what the Glibb sales rep, who happened to be around when this occurred, told you. She said that ABC was "known to do this type of thing." You are furious and almost ready to forget all of ABC's products, even though some of their products are clearly superior.

Lee has requested to see you this afternoon. You agreed to the meeting because you like her — she really knows her stuff — and the fact that you have known her for several years. You would like to continue the lower pricing schedule but know this will not be an easy objective to achieve.

Note:

ABC sells three other products to Staunton, but pricing on these is not in question.

LEE STONE
Sales Representative

Joe Kirk is the Purchasing Agent at Staunton Stationery. Staunton is a medium sized organization, but growing, and is one of your better clients. You and Joe have always had a good relationship.

When you called Joe last week to give him the new price of B-1 Forms, he almost hit the roof, saying he would pay only the same price ($6.85 per hundred) that he'd paid for the last two years. When you questioned him about this price, you found that he has been purchasing the forms through a state-wide buying group at a substantial savings. These forms and those of your competitor's (Glibb) are about the same, but you have clearly been outselling Glibb at Staunton.

When you checked into this with Contract Sales, you found that Staunton has been ordering B-1 Forms through a state-wide buying group at $6.85 per hundred — more than 50% off the bid price. This was through our own error and has been going on for at least the past two years. It's no wonder that Joe exploded when you quoted him a price of $15.25 per hundred. You'd be upset too!

To complicate matters, the Glibb sales rep got wind of this situation and told Joe that, "ABC is known for doing that kind of thing; that's the way they operate." This just isn't true, it was an honest mistake. In spite of your assurances, Joe is understandably upset and has threatened to sign on with Glibb, even though their price is comparable to your quoted price. Your guess is that he made the threat on the spur of the moment and isn't really serious. He is, however, clearly upset.

You spoke with your boss and Contract Sales. Everyone agrees that Joe has to be gotten onto the correct pricing schedule as quickly as possible, but have left it up to you as to how this should be accomplished. Contract Sales even feels that we should back charge him for everything he received at the lower price. You don't see this as possible, but it's a sign of how upset people are about the situation. In fact, Marketing has asked that a review be made of all the national and local buying groups to make sure that this isn't happening with others.

Note:

You have a meeting set up with Joe in a few minutes. You sell three other products to Staunton, but pricing on these is not in question.

Title:	**THE GARAGE SALE**	**#4**

Time:	Twenty Minutes

Objectives:	To illustrate:

- the importance of planning

- the fact that there is no right answer in negotiation

- the importance of high aspirations

Trainer Note:	This is a fun role play. It's a good one to use early in a program.

Introduction:	For this negotiation to be effective, it is important to do a brief lecture on planning prior to the negotiation. In this lecture you should include some methodology for rating importance of objectives. Any format is acceptable, as long as it is something people are comfortable with. Then ask the participants to develop settlement options. For example, they might pay a different price for a package deal than for individual items. Tell people they can keep this plan with them during the negotiation.

Before beginning, reemphasize that they can buy or sell as many or as few items as they want.

Debriefing Note:	To get maximum benefit from this negotiation, the following format is suggested.

After everyone is finished:

- Go around the room and ask people if they are satisfied. Do not allow them to say more than "Yes" or "No."

- Ask why they are satisfied. Most will indicate that they achieved their objective.

- Ask how helpful the planning was in achieving their objectives. Ask: In what way was the planning helpful? Did you look at your plan during the negotiation? Most will have found the planning critical to their success.

- Summarize key points. Highlight the relationship between the planning and achieving one's objective.

- After the discussion is completed, ask for the settlements. Make sure to note special issues — delivery, etc.

- *Post results.*

- After all results are posted, ask for the significance of the diverse settlements. Usually there is great diversity and participants will realize that there is no right answer. For instance, sometimes buyers will spend all their money for the piano and will indicate they are also happy with the outcome.

- The right answer is a function of our objectives and aspirations.

Summary: Do a brief lecture on the importance and value of planning and being clear beforehand about objectives and possible settlements.

You noted an advertisement in the paper listing a piano, oriental style carpet, and wooden desk for sale. The piano attracted your attention since you have wanted to buy one for your spouse for some time. However, you just haven't been able to find the right one at the right price. Your spouse has been talking about resuming his/her career as a professional pianist and having a piano at home to practice on would help him/her get beyond the talking stage.

Although you really want the piano, you are not overly interested in the other two items. They probably could be used in your office, but you're not sure. Nor are you too sure how your spouse would react to your buying them. If the price is right, the piano is no problem since both of you have talked about it, even about where it would fit in your apartment.

You are now at the seller's home to look over the merchandise. As you enter the room you notice the piano which seems to be in excellent condition. All the other pianos you have seen didn't look half as good. You quickly decide that you would be willing to pay up to $750.00.

The desk would probably work in your office at home, but it's scratched and is water stained. Otherwise it seems to be in pretty good condition, and you would be willing to pay as much as $325.00.

The carpet also looks in pretty good shape, but is dirty and needs cleaning. It too would look good in the office and you would be willing to pay $225.00.

You have $1,300.00 to spend.

You have just been asked by a friend who has taken a job in another city to sell all the remaining furniture in his apartment. Three pieces are left. They are:

- An upright piano about 10 years old and in good condition. It was made by one of the best piano makers and was tuned only two months ago. You would like to get $600.00 for it.
- A wooden desk that was made to order. It is in pretty good condition but is scratched in several spots and has several stains from wet glasses. You would like to get $250.00 for it.
- A 9x12 oriental style carpet purchased in Greece four years ago. It is a good one with a very deep, rich pile, made by one of the best carpet makers in Greece. It is in good condition and would probably look like new after a cleaning. You would like $200.00 for it.

In your friend's letter he said that he didn't know how much everything was worth but wanted to net at least $500.00 for all three pieces. He indicated that he would split 50/50 with you everything you can get over $500.00. He will also reimburse you for any out-of-pocket expenses.

You placed an advertisement in a local paper for all three pieces without indicating the price. You received several responses; one from someone who sounded very interested. You have an appointment with that person in about 5 minutes.

Title:	**THE WORK REQUEST**	**#5**

Time:	Thirty Minutes
Objective:	To practice the Six Step Model of negotiation.
Trainer Note:	This role play is ideal in looking at negotiations among departments. It can be used with any group.
Debriefing Note:	To successfully complete this practice negotiation, it is critical that the person playing Lee Stone explore the underlying needs and interests of Dana Kent. If this becomes a negotiation over Dale Clark, it will become very difficult to complete. Dale represents "security" to Dana and there are a variety of ways this "security" can be provided without using Dale to do the work. Typical of the solutions on this issue are: Dale supervises Elaine, Dale does some work up front, or that he come in at the conclusion of the project to review it.

Many times the people playing Lee will realize the importance of Dale to Dana, but do not acknowledge to Dana they have heard his/her concern. Participants must realize that they need to hear the other party's concerns and then acknowledge their understanding of them.

Usually the "Dale as security" issue needs to be dealt with first, since it's so important to Dana. Once that is accomplished, the other issues are much easier to resolve.

During the debriefing ask how many people explored options other than utilizing Dale during their planning and what impact this had on the negotiation.

Your department needs a financial reporting system designed as soon as possible. You need to have the capability to do a number of things:

- track foreign currency fluctuations and their impact on cash flow;
- generate financial reports;
- do financial forecasting.

If possible, you also want the ability to present data graphically; this would greatly enhance the system.

You have a meeting schedule with Lee Stone of M.I.S. to discuss both your needs and the assignment of someone to handle the job for you. You chatted briefly with Lee this morning and outlined your basic needs, although you didn't go into great detail.

The job must be completed in no more than two months, so that you can be ready for the new fiscal year which is three months away. However, your preference would be to finish the job in six weeks, which would give you the cushion you need to cover the problems which invariably occur on these jobs. You also want the time to train your staff and to run several tests of the system.

You would like Lee to assign Dale Clark, with whom you worked several years ago on a similar project. You know that Dale has the ability to turn out a top notch job within four to six weeks. In fact, you heard that he recently was promoted to supervisor.

You called Dale about this last week and he said that it sounded like an interesting assignment and, if the people "up top" agreed, he would have no objection to doing it.

You don't want M.I.S. to give you one of their new "hot shots," since you know they won't do half the job Dale will and would probably take a lot longer, going beyond your two month deadline. You don't want this job to be used as part of anyone's "on-the-job-training" — let them do that on a less important assignment. This assignment is critical and is a highly visible project.

You have enough in your budget to pay for this job, but since M.I.S. always wants to call all the shots, you feel that they should pay for the whole thing. You want to begin work immediately because this would get several people, including your boss, off your back. It will also ensure that your deadline is met, and will send a message to everyone that work is underway.

You haven't had a great deal of contact with Lee, but that which you've had has generally been positive.

Dana Kent of International Accounting called you this morning to discuss their need for a new financial reporting system. Dana didn't go into a great deal of detail, he only said that he would like to talk with you.

The design of this system doesn't sound difficult, in fact, it sounds like one that could be completed by one of your newer people in no more than two months. However, you'd like to get more time if you can — it would make life a lot easier. This assignment will provide the kind of exposure that you want your new people to have and it will give them an opportunity to function as a consultant to another department. It's a good developmental assignment.

You have Elaine Stewart in mind for the assignment, although she couldn't begin for at least two weeks. Elaine has a good technical background as well as the type of people skills necessary to work with Accounting. You don't want to assign one of your more senior people to the job since it wouldn't be an effective use of your staff. Elaine has been at the company for about 8 months and has completed several assignments very successfully. Prior to joining the company she worked for a major bank, so she is very familiar with financial systems.

You believe that Dana may want Dale Clark to do this job, since Accounting was very pleased with the work he did several years ago on a similar project. However, Dale was promoted to a supervisory position about seven months ago and no longer designs this kind of system. However, he still reports to you.

Knowing the folks in Accounting, they're going to want you to cover a significant portion, if not all, of the cost of the job. Then they'll let everyone know how they got you to give them what they wanted. You'd like them to assume their fair share of the cost of the system, even though you could easily cover it. Like most people, they usually overstate how quickly they need something done.

You haven't had a lot of contact with Dana, but that which you have had has always been positive.

Title:	**PURCHASING PROBLEM** #6
Time:	Thirty Minutes
Objectives:	To negotiate the internal roles and responsibilities of the Purchasing Officer. To conduct a negotiation in which time is a significant variable. To discuss the implications of working in a boundary role function.
Trainer Note:	This role play is excellent for illustrating the Successful Negotiator Model. It is ideal when used with a purchasing department. Although set in a research facility, it is general enough to work with any purchasing group. If you decide to look at boundary role issues, see the Trainer Note in Role Play #7.
Debriefing Note:	As with Role Play #5, talking about needs and interests will be critical to a successful outcome. The only way the parties can achieve a workable, long term solution is if these are surfaced and discussed. Also, it is important to explore how Mike addressed Pam's immediate concern and her problems with her boss. Failure to do that will serve to make the negotiation quite difficult. Mike must demonstrate a real understanding of Pam's needs. Pam usually will not let Mike talk about the overall relationship if he has not assured her that the immediate problem can be solved without putting her in jeopardy with her boss. The issue portrayed is very typical for most purchasing groups and can serve as a stimulus for a discussion of how to deal with it.

You are a buyer with responsibility for the research labs. It is a job you enjoy, and one that you feel well qualified to handle. You were a buyer at both ACMP and Beta, and had responsibility at both companies for the labs. More importantly, you were seen as a resource at both firms, with people usually coming to you for advice and assistance. You understand that it's not your job to decide on what equipment is needed, but to ensure that terms and conditions are fair to both the company and the supplier. However here, more frequently than not, people come to you with their minds made up and just want you to do the paperwork. Typical of what happens is this:

Pam Stone called you last week with a requisition for an electron microscope that she wanted you to take care of. She had already met with the vendor's sales rep, who convinced her that she was getting "the best available price" and that if she ordered by next Wednesday, he could assure delivery within seven days. However, if the order isn't placed by then, delivery would take at least 3 weeks. Pam went on to point out that she knew the product, that it was the best one available and that she didn't have any time to waste since she needs the equipment as soon as possible. You didn't argue with her, since you were involved with a dozen other things at the time. You told her, "just send the requisition and I'll take care of it."

When the requisition arrived, you saw who the vendor was and decided to call the sales rep in an effort to get a better price. You have dealt with this company in the past (although not with this rep) and know they have flexibility on price and delivery, especially for large customers. We are one of their largest, and it's time to begin receiving volume discounts. At your old firm you received discounts for less volume.

You called the sales rep earlier this morning to discuss the order. He was not happy. About twenty minutes ago you received a call from Pam, who was really upset. She asked what you were up to. The sales rep had just called and told her that you wanted to negotiate price. She said that there was no need to do so, they had already agreed on price and she needed the microscope immediately. "Moreover," she said, "I have the necessary money in my budget, so let's not make a federal case out of this — just get the paperwork completed and get the scope ordered."

You suggested that you meet to discuss what was happening. She was not overjoyed at the prospect, but agreed to meet.

As you think about the problem, you know that you can save the company money, and not cause any delivery problems. This sales rep has done his job well, bypassing you and convincing the end user that only if the order is placed immediately can price and delivery be assured. You know that there is flexibility on price and for a company like yours, the delivery schedule can be met regardless of when the order is placed.

Your own problem is how to convince Pam to let you "do your thing," especially since she has the money budgeted and the rep knows it. You are annoyed that Pam would think that you would somehow mess things up. It's as if it's you against Pam and the rep. That's *not* the way it should be. How do you tell one of your senior research people that she is certainly not a negotiator, and in fact, has been "taken" by a smart sales rep?

You are to meet with Pam in fifteen minutes.

Why don't these people in Purchasing let you do your job? You just got a call from Ed Mann, the sales rep for Ventri Manufacturing. You and he had worked out a purchase of their new electron microscope, which he promised could be delivered in seven days, if the Purchase Order was submitted by week's end.

As far as you're concerned, this was a real favor, since you had been sitting on this for some three weeks after your boss asked you to take care of it. Even better was his coming in just under budget. You told Ed how much you had to spend and he didn't hold you up for a higher price — which he surely could have. This is typical of Ed and you appreciate that kind of service. If only Purchasing did the same thing. Don't they understand their job? It's not their responsibility to tell you what or from whom to purchase. When you need something ordered, their job is to do the paperwork so that the goods show up on time. In the past, no matter when you placed the order, Purchasing got the paperwork done, although they complained occasionally about how little time you gave them. You always promised to do better, but nothing really changed.

When you talked with Ed, he said that if he had to go through Purchasing, delivery would probably be delayed and the price raised, because of the added paperwork and time involved.

You talked with Mike Brown in Purchasing and sent him the paperwork last week. You expected that everything would be taken care of — especially since you explained how important the equipment was and how helpful the rep had been — coming in under budget and ensuring quick delivery. Mike never indicated that there would be a problem, so you assumed that it would be business as usual. However, early this morning the rep called you indicating that "Mike Brown from Purchasing" had called him, asking to discuss your order. When you asked Ed what he meant, he indicated that "Mike wanted to discuss price and delivery." He went on to say that he was troubled by this, since "when you and I shake hands, that's it." He asked what he should do and you said that you would call Mike and get back to him. You called

Mike — really upset — and told him to leave this alone and not to screw up the good relationship you have with Ed. Now he wants to meet with you to "discuss what is happening."

As you sit and think about this problem, you remember how many times Ed Mann has come through for you in the past. He knows his job. You don't want to do anything that will rock the boat and you surely don't want anything to affect this order. Maybe if you had taken care of it right away — but not now. Your boss asked about it earlier this week and you said that there would be no problem — everything was under control. Your boss expects that the scope will be delivered within the next five days. No problem! These are your boss' favorite words and he doesn't like to be disappointed. You just want to get this order taken care of, even if you have to do all the paperwork yourself!

Mike is probably upset by the requisition coming in so late and with your manner on the phone. You really did get carried away! It's for this reason that you agreed to meet with him.

You also want to clarify that you really know what you want and need and that there is no need for him to get so involved.

That meeting will begin in about fifteen minutes.

Mike (Purchasing) and Pam (Research) know each other, but are not great friends.

It is now Wednesday morning.

Pam has selected a vendor for an electron microscope and has worked out a price that was within her budget.

The vendor agreed to a one week delivery, if the paperwork was in by Wednesday.

Pam asked Mike to take care of the paperwork, based on the price and delivery schedule agreed to with the vendor.

Mike called the sales rep to discuss price.

Mike and Pam talked several months ago about getting in requisitions earlier to give Purchasing more time. Things improved, but then went back to "business as usual."

Pam got this requisition to Mike last Friday morning.

Pam and Mike spoke several minutes ago and Pam blew up on the phone.

Title:	**THE BOUNDARY ROLE**	**#7**

Time:	Twenty Minutes

Objectives:	To practice all the steps in the negotiating process.
	To discuss the implications of working in a boundary role function.

Trainer Note:	This role play as written is best used with pharmaceutical companies, and is ideally suited for homogeneous groups that work in boundary roles.
	This negotiation should be used in conjunction with a discussion of the Boundary Role Concept.
	There are several good articles on boundary role issues. They are:

- Fobian, Cynthia (1987). *Interorganizational Negotiation and Accountability: An Examination of the Adams' Paradox.* The article can be purchased from the National Institute of Dispute Resolution, 1900 L Street N.W., Washington, D.C. 20030.

- Adams, J.S. (1976). "The Structure and Dynamics of Behavior in Organizational Boundary Roles." In M.E. Donette (Ed.), *Handbook of Industrial and Organizational Psychology.* Chicago: Rand McNally.

Debriefing Note:	In debriefing this role you will find that many groups will focus only on the content and will not talk at all about their relationship. They will offer a variety of excuses for not doing so.
	If this happens, it is important to discuss the implications of not discussing these issues. As a second step you should talk about how these issues can be raised without negatively affecting the relationship.

If your group is primarily made up of boundary role people, you should discuss the concept of boundary roles, the conflicts that they raise, and what steps can be taken to resolve these conflicts. The central issue is the conflict between the demands of our internal constituents and the outside groups that we need to deal with. It is critical in this discussion to talk about participants' real life experiences and how these issues can be resolved. The articles listed in the Trainer Note will be helpful in this regard.

You work in the Regulatory Liaison division of your company and your job is such that you spend much of your time interfacing with the FDA. This is a job that you have held for several years, both here and at another company. You enjoy your work and feel that you have built a good reputation with the FDA. They know you to be honest. You don't take shortcuts. Your approach has and always will be to develop a strong relationship with your FDA counterpart built on trust and cooperation. Your philosophy is that your job is to represent your company and to be a strong advocate for the company's position, but within an appropriate professional framework. However, sometimes it seems as if the better your working relationship is with the agency, the less credible you become to your coworkers. This makes your internal negotiations more difficult.

You are now faced with a difficult choice. What you are now being asked to do can only jeopardize all that you have worked so hard to develop. One of your areas — Anti-Infectives — wants you to arrange a meeting with the FDA to push one of their newer compounds, C-259. You are uncomfortable with this, since you don't believe the science is there on this drug. Although the regulatory requirements for AIDS drugs are far from being defined by the FDA, Clinical and Marketing see only the political advantage and fail to recognize the potential for a broader impact on company/FDA relations. You can appreciate that the AIDS issue provides a window of opportunity, but you don't think that this should be an excuse for poor science. The data just isn't there on this compound, but you wouldn't know that from the way people are behaving. As one of the business people said to you recently:

"Look, there's a real opportunity with these anti-infective compounds. With all the concern about AIDS, the government is finally being forced to become realistic in its approach to drug approval. I know that the science isn't all there, but at this point that isn't an issue. The drug isn't dangerous and the initial data suggest it can be helpful, both with AIDS and with other infections. Furthermore, several of the AIDS groups are interested in this drug and I know we can move it along. This is an opportunity we can't let pass by."

You are not convinced that the FDA will simply give us the go-ahead. While they're clearly under pressure, they are distinctly uncomfortable with what is happening. In fact, several people have said to you, off the record, that they feel a very bad precedent is being established by the rapid approval process.

You are also concerned that Clinical expects that the political pressure on the FDA to expedite the development of AIDS drugs means not only faster approvals based on less data, but the opportunity to do "sloppy" work. This isn't something you feel comfortable with. Your preference would be to talk informally with your contacts at the FDA to get some guidance and a sense of what they're looking for before any big meetings are held. You know that your boss sees this issue the same way.

You have a meeting scheduled with the Anti-Infective people shortly to discuss the next steps. You also plan to bring up the issue of how they see your role and your general relationship, not only with the FDA, but agencies world-wide.

You have a meeting scheduled shortly with Sally Jones from Regulatory Liaison to discuss her reluctance to move ahead on C-259. You aren't sure you understand the people in Liaison — don't they know their job is to represent the company and see that we get compounds approved?

You work in the Anti-Infectives area and it's become very exciting lately — there are real opportunities. With the public concern about AIDS and the pressure to find effective drugs, the government is becoming far more lenient in allowing companies to begin testing new compounds. This is a window of opportunity that isn't likely to come along again anytime soon and we need to take advantage of it.

Anti-Infectives has a brand new compound — C-259 — that you want to get into the FDA pipeline as soon as possible. It's a good drug and you know the government will give you the go-ahead. However, your biggest problem these days isn't the FDA but Liaison. They keep insisting that the science — the data — isn't there and that we do ourselves a disservice if we go to the FDA with "flimsy" data. You have some preliminary safety and efficacy data, but all the results have not yet been processed. You probably haven't collected all the available data on this one and you're making some "educated guesses," but the FDA seems to understand that this sort of thing has to happen if AIDS drugs are to be developed and get to market quickly. So should your own people, they're the real problem. In fact, they're probably behind the FDA in their view of the world. You've gotten support from other departments for this approach; they also find the position that Liaison is taking to be obstructive.

Sometimes you get the feeling that Liaison is more concerned with satisfying the FDA than with getting our drugs approved. It frequently seems like they're working for the FDA and not for the company. Your previous company was much more aggressive in dealing with the FDA and as a result, you believe they were much more successful in getting drugs approved.

You want Liaison to set up a meeting at the FDA and you would like this meeting sooner, rather than later. In addition, either you or your boss want to be at the meeting — but preferably both of you. You understand better than anyone exactly what you have and can be most effective in explaining the preliminary results. You know you can get the green light from the agency!

You will meet with Sally shortly to discuss this issue.

Title:	**THE PURCHASING ROLE** **#8**
Time:	Thirty Minutes
Objective:	To provide an opportunity to negotiate the role of Purchasing within the organization.
Trainer Note:	This negotiation is ideal for use with purchasing groups, with departments that do a great deal of work with Purchasing, or with both groups together.
	This role play can also be effective in exploring the boundary role concept mentioned in Role Play #7.
Debriefing Note:	In debriefing this negotiation, it is important to explore the degree to which the parties surfaced each others' underlying needs and interests. The only way they can achieve a workable, long term solution is if these are surfaced and discussed.
	Dana has an existing relationship with a supplier. It is important that this be surfaced and that Dana is assured that the relationship will not be damaged.
	In addition, they need to discuss their current perceptions of each other, as well as their roles and responsibilities.
	Explore the behaviors that allowed these issues to be discussed.
	As with Role Play #7, if you discuss the boundary role issue, you should discuss the conflicts and concerns it raises, how to resolve these issues, and possible solutions.

You have always liked the people in Purchasing; they are always ready to expedite your requests. Their system works like a charm. If you need a particular piece of equipment, you first meet with a vendor to work out the details and then send the paperwork to the appropriate buyer. Unless there is some problem, the equipment always shows up when it's supposed to.

This procedure works real well for you; you've been in the business quite some time and know what you need. In fact, you don't need much, if any, help from Purchasing. You have the budget, you know the vendors, and your boss has given you the authority to make the needed purchases. When compared to your previous company, this is a real pleasure. Where you previously worked, the Purchasing people were always looking to be involved "up front," working with you to get the "best deal." As a result, you didn't always get exactly what you wanted and the process took much longer. In addition, you doubt that they got a better price. Your experience with Purchasing is that they're too concerned with price.

Last week, one of the buyers, Lee Larson, called asking for a meeting. When you asked about what, Lee said he wanted to discuss how they could work with you in the coming fiscal year. You hate to even think about what this might mean! You have several major purchases coming up in the next year and have already begun discussions with several vendors. The biggest purchase will be for a computer system, along with all the software and new printers. This purchase alone will be upwards of $300,000. You are not sure how much Lee knows about the upcoming purchases, but you have no doubt he's heard something through the grapevine. Right now, nothing is an emergency, but you want to make a decision about the system in several weeks. This shouldn't present a problem. While there are several good manufacturers, you would prefer to deal with Vax Technologies, a relatively small firm that makes a great computer. You've worked with Vax in the past and their equipment is reliable. Equally important is their sales rep — Janet Vincent. You and she have been talking about computer systems for at least three months, even before you and your boss decided to buy one. You know and like Janet; service is her key. You have a large conference coming up in several weeks and you can't afford to be bothered with the details of equipment delivery and installation. You know that Janet is willing and able to take care of all that for you in your absence.

And, while you haven't begun any discussion on the other equipment purchases, you have ideas about the companies you want to work with. Allowing Purchasing to get involved only promises to complicate matters and upset relationships you already have.

As you think about this meeting, you'd really like to keep Lee out of the process. You like the current arrangements — you decide and Lee takes care of the paperwork. Maybe you'll be lucky and that's all he wants to talk about — especially since you anticipate an additional $250,000 worth of expenditures, not counting the computers, during the rest of the fiscal year.

You mentioned Lee's call to your boss and he said that you should do whatever makes you feel comfortable.

You are about to meet with Lee. Take the next several minutes to prepare for the meeting.

Known to Both Parties

Dana and Lee know each other.

In the past, when Manufacturing bought equipment, they made the decisions pretty much on their own. Purchasing was involved only to ensure that the correct paperwork was processed.

You are tired of being everyone's clerk! You are a professional, although you doubt that anyone outside of the department realizes the full range of your skills. In the present system of purchasing equipment, almost every line manager determines what they need, contacts the vendor, agrees on a price, and then asks you or one of your coworkers to take care of the paperwork.

For the most part, you have done what they've requested — especially since everyone in your department was so busy that you couldn't have gotten involved up front, even if you wanted to. However, now that more time is available and everyone is feeling less put upon, you have decided that this isn't the way you want to do business.

In reviewing your purchase orders for the past year, it became clear to you that the company could have saved a great deal of money in some of the major equipment purchases if you had been involved earlier. As a first step, you have set up a meeting with Dana Kent in Manufacturing to explain how you would like to proceed in the future and try to get his/her buy-in. When Dana asked what the meeting would be about, you said that you wanted "to discuss how you could work with him/her in the coming fiscal year." He did not sound overjoyed! This meeting is particularly important for you since you heard that Manufacturing will be buying some new equipment next year. Although you are not clear on exactly what they intend to purchase, you've heard that they are looking at a number of computers. Considering all the ancillary equipment, this can cost upwards of $300,000. There are several companies on the market that have the necessary computers. This is something you've been involved with previously and you know there is usually a lot of room to negotiate on price and service. This is especially true if you could consolidate your purchases from several departments with one or two firms. The company is already buying a number of items from Apex, who sell and service a variety of excellent systems, and you know they would be very flexible on price — they're looking to build a relationship with us. Knowing the people in Manufacturing, you wouldn't be surprised if they've already made their decision. As you think about how the company is expanding, it wouldn't surprise you if you were looking at a total of close to $600,000 worth of new equipment purchases for the Manufacturing group next year. This is the ideal time for you to work with Dana to demonstrate what Purchasing can do!

You will meet with Dana in fifteen minutes. Take the next several minutes to prepare for the negotiation.

Known to Both Parties

Dana and Lee know each other.

In the past, when Manufacturing bought equipment, they made the decisions pretty much on their own. Purchasing was involved only to ensure that the correct paperwork was processed.

| *Title:* | **CONSULTANT** | **#9** |

| *Time:* | Fifteen Minutes |

| *Objectives:* | To illustrate the importance of Issue Identification. |

| | To practice establishing impartial standards as a vehicle for clarifying issues. |

| *Trainer Note:* | This negotiation is ideal for clinical research and marketing groups in the pharmaceutical industry. |

| | See Chapter Five in the Fisher and Ury book, *Getting to Yes;* there is an excellent discussion of establishing objective criteria as a vehicle for solving negotiation problems. |

| | This role play works one of two ways. In most groups, participants list the reasons for wanting their consultant. In others they seek to establish a standard against which to judge both candidates. This will usually come about after they have experienced frustration with discussing their individual choices. If they do not establish objective criteria, you should raise it with the group. In the context of this negotiation, the objective criteria could include being a good speaker, doing good research, and having previously worked for the company. |

| *Debriefing Note:* | Make sure to surface any differences in the approaches used in clarifying issues and the impact they will have on the remainder of the negotiation. |

ABC recently purchased the rights to develop a new antihistamine — called Compound A. We are particularly interested in this compound because it complements our current family of drugs.

Before the purchase, Marketing did the basic research on Compound A and found that it could be very profitable and helpful to allergy sufferers. Mike Sappor in Clinical Research is the Project Leader. The initial Phase III studies are scheduled to begin in two months. Everyone on the project team is enthused and excited about the possibilities for Compound A.

Both you and John Fletcher in Sales feel that the pivotal studies should be conducted by Dr. Malcolm Coleman of the State University. Dr. Coleman is the best known researcher in the field and has many studies to his credit. To be able to publish an article by him would be a real coup and would almost ensure immediate acceptance by the medical community. In addition, Dr. Coleman is an outstanding speaker and will usually make himself available for seminars and presentations. He's always easy to work with on Marketing issues.

The only problem is Mike Sappor in Clinical Research. They've worked with Dr. Coleman and feel that he's too much of a "prima donna" to use on a study as important as this one. Instead, they want to use a woman at Western — someone you've never heard of before — Dr. Katherine Stone. She may know her stuff, but her name will be of no marketing value. Sometimes you think that all your explanations about Marketing's needs during project team meetings simply fall on deaf ears!

You are about to meet with Mike Sappor to discuss this with him. You are anxious to resolve this problem.

Your company recently purchased the rights to Compound A, a new antihistamine. Compound A is particularly interesting, since it complements our current family of drugs. As Project Leader you are excited about its prospects. From the Marketing and Phase II studies, it looks as if it will be a real winner. You've requested additional CRA support on this project in an effort to get it through Phase III as quickly and efficiently as possible.

Last week, you got a call from Bob Davidson over in Marketing. He was urging that Dr. Malcolm Coleman be used as the primary investigator on the pivotal studies. Bob feels that Coleman's reputation and the prestige of his University will be helpful in marketing the drug. You are opposed to Coleman — the last study he ran for you was a disaster. Dr. Coleman may have a great reputation, but his administrative skills are terrible. He rarely gets the project data in on time and he often doesn't have any idea of what his staff is doing. You have another person in mind — Dr. Katherine Stone from Western. You have used her on several projects over the past several years and found her to be exceptional. She may not have the reputation of Coleman, but she's much more dependable — something you need on a study as important as this one. If she's interested in Compound A — and there's no reason that she wouldn't be — you want to use her. You anticipate some trouble, or at least an argument, from Marketing on this. Their own concern is marketing the drug — even though that's several years down the road. They could care less about the problems of doing the research!

You are meeting with Bob in a few minutes to discuss this — although you really are not sure there's anything to discuss.

Title:	**THE GUEST SPEAKER**	**#10**

Time:	Fifteen Minutes
Objectives:	To practice the steps in Issue Identification.
	To demonstrate the importance of Issue Identification.
Trainer Note:	This is an excellent role play for illustrating how Issue Identification can solve the problem.
	When done correctly, the solution will usually come about when the parties realize they have no disagreement and, by clarifying the issues, have solved the problem. While their difference is clearly about Dr. Fletcher, Sally has only seen her in front of large groups where she is ineffective. Rick knows this and, as a result, is going to use her in a smaller, more informal setting.
Debriefing Note:	• Determine which groups did only Issue Identification and which went into Bargaining. Ask: "What happened to the groups that went into bargaining? Of the groups that did Issue Identification, how many found that this solved the problem?"
	• Have these groups talk about how it solved the problem and what they did well.
	• Reconfirm the importance of Issue Identification and how, if done well, may solve the problem.

SALLY NIBERG
Vice President, Marketing

You are about to go into a meeting with Rick Sanders, the Western Division Marketing Manager. Rick has requested this meeting to discuss your refusal to okay a speaker for next year's company-sponsored Software Conference. You feel that his person — Dr. Martha Fletcher — is not the best choice for the presentation. You wish that Sales would talk to you before they plan these things. You are familiar with speakers and could have told him that even though Dr. Fletcher is a prominent figure, she's not a good speaker. In fact, on the two times you used her, she was not good. Since both times were before large prestigious groups, it was very embarrassing for you. In fact, the second time you consented to use her — against your better judgment.

You agreed to meet with Rick today, even though your schedule is hectic. The conference is six months away, but this needs to be settled as soon as possible. Rick sent the request to you several weeks ago, but you didn't get to it until last week because of your travel schedule. You and Rick have often disagreed — even quarreled — over budgets. It seems that he always wants more than you can give, both in money and in staff. Like most department heads, he's always pushing for his people and doesn't always see the big picture. Rick is probably still unhappy about not getting the extra office support he requested from you several weeks ago. His attitude sometimes annoys you. He always comes off sounding superior. You are sure that he's annoyed because you turned down Dr. Fletcher. This puts you in a difficult situation — you don't like turning programs down! It's not good for you, your people, or the department. You would like to get this immediate problem solved, as well as establish a procedure that will involve you sooner in planning meetings, so this doesn't happen again.

RICK SANDERS
Western Division Marketing Manager

You are about to go into a meeting with Sally Niberg, the Marketing Vice President for your region. You just about hit the roof last week when Sally turned down a budget request for a small, company-sponsored Software Conference to be held next year. You suspect that Sally left the request sitting on her desk for several weeks and now has decided that it costs too much. Although the conference is to be held in six months, it presents an urgent situation since the program must be in place within two weeks.

This situation is especially difficult, since you consider this program to be very important and have worked very hard getting Dr. Martha Fletcher, a nationally known software expert, to speak. You originally thought you should capitalize on her reputation by having a larger group, but you learned that she is only good with small groups. Dr. Fletcher is just not effective in front of large groups where the presentation is much more formal. She tends to get nervous. This small group is ideal for her.

You requested a meeting with Sally to try to get her to approve the request, but you've had trouble with her in the past. It took long hours of discussion before she would approve your discretionary marketing budget in the first place, yet she's very quick to complain that your people are not devoting enough time to outside causes. In addition, just last month she told you that you couldn't have the part-time help that you felt you needed.

It will really create problems if Sally doesn't approve this speaker. Plans have already been made with Dr. Fletcher and a lot of important people are looking forward to this meeting — she is very well respected.

You want to get this issue ironed out without jeopardizing your relationship with Sally and see that it does not happen again.

Sally is a Marketing Vice President. Rick is Western Division Marketing Manager.

In a telephone conversation earlier this week, Sally indicated that she would not approve the request for a company-sponsored speaker's program. Rick asked for this meeting as a result of the phone conversation.

| Title: | **DAMAGED GOODS** | **#11** |

| Time: | Twenty-five Minutes |

| Objectives: | To practice the Six Step Model of negotiation. |
| | To discuss how to deal with a customer problem. |

| Trainer Note: | This is a good role play for teaching how to deal with a legitimate customer complaint. It also provides a nice jumping off point for a discussion of customer service. |

| Debriefing Notes: | To effectively solve this problem, it is critical that Issue Identification be well done and that the sales rep acknowledge, not diminish, the client's concern. In your debriefing, focus on the behaviors utilized by the sales rep. |
| | After the discussion has been completed, discuss how your company deals with customer complaints and what its experience has been. |

You have dealt with Krystall, a European crystal company, for the past ten years. They are a good company, providing quality items which have always sold well in your stores.

As with all glass, there has sometimes been a problem with breakage. In the past you have absorbed the expense. You mentioned the breakage problem to Sam, Krystall's U.S. rep, about six months ago, but he put you off, saying that the merchandise could have been damaged in the warehouse and that unless someone had checked it upon arrival, he couldn't help. He went on to suggest that in the future you have the shipments checked upon arrival. This is difficult to do since you often purchase several months' supply, and most of it is moved directly to inventory without being opened. However, when Krystall's shipment arrived last week, you had it spot checked immediately and found that over 10% was chipped or broken. With all the new mandates about cost reduction and departmental profit centers, you need to get agreement on Sam's part to do something about merchandise that arrives in damaged condition. He very clearly needs to do something about this order; it is unacceptable.

You called Sam and asked him to meet you today. You are about to begin your meeting.

Known to Both Parties

Toni is a Senior Buyer for Glass Etc.

Sam is the Krystall Sales Rep.

Toni has never really complained about this problem before.

Glass Etc. is one of your best accounts. Not only do they move your merchandise well, but Toni, the buyer, is a great person to deal with.

However, over the past year and a half there have been some problems with damaged merchandise arriving on the selling floor. When Toni complained, you told her that since the merchandise may have become damaged in their warehouse, you couldn't be held responsible for it. You suggested that they check goods immediately upon arrival, never expecting that they would follow your advice.

Glass' latest shipment arrived at the warehouse several days ago. Yesterday, Toni called and said she wanted to talk to you. You're afraid that they are going to become like all the other stores — complaining about every little detail. You don't intend to begin a situation where half of every order is returned become some guy in the warehouse thinks he sees something wrong with it. There is always some breakage with crystal, and Toni knows that.

You have spoken with your boss about this issue and she indicated that you should do whatever is necessary. To quote her, "Glass is too important. They haven't complained in the past and we don't want to lose them. Do what you have to do, but within reason: Use your best judgment."

Known to Both Parties

Toni is a Senior Buyer for Glass Etc.

Sam is the Krystall Sales Rep.

Toni has never complained about this problem before.

Title:	**THE ANTIQUE CAR**	**#12**

Time:	Ten Minutes
Objective:	To illustrate the importance of process to the success of a negotiation.
Trainer Note:	This negotiation should be used early in a program. Most participants will complete this role play very quickly. Frequently, some groups do not follow the directions and a more elaborate negotiation will begin.
Debriefing Note:	In conducting the debriefing, determine the groups in which the seller asked for $160,000 and received it immediately.

- Ask the sellers how they feel. *(Most will not be happy.)*

- Ask why they feel as they do. What is missing? Didn't they get what they asked for?

- If they got what they wanted, ask why they are upset.

- Ask if anyone has experienced this feeling in real life.

After the discussion, do a brief lecture on the distinction between content and process. *(Content focuses on what we are negotiating, the process is on the how.)* Point out that for a negotiation to be successful, it is important that both the content and process be right. If either is missing, one of the parties may feel emotionally cheated and that they did a poor job as a negotiator. Usually, if people do not feel good about how they performed, they will not feel committed to the deal. The less committed, the greater the potential that they will look for a way out. If the content and process are right, there will be an emotional commitment to the deal and its implementation.

Conclusion: It is important that you help participants transfer the Content/Process concept to their job. We suggest that you lead a brief discussion on how to increase satisfaction. Focus on process issues, not content. Typical of the items people will mention are:

- Give people time.

- Listen to them.

- Ask questions.

- Demonstrate empathy.

- Ask for other opinions.

Because of financial problems you are being forced to dispose of part of your antique car collection. This is not something you are excited about doing. You love your cars and it has taken you a long time to build your collection.

Last week you advertised one of your 1926 Rolls Royce Silver Clouds for sale. These were the ultimate Rolls Royce cars. Because of time constraints, you have not checked on their exact current market value. However, your plan is to ask for *$160,000.00*, which is what similar cars have sold for during the past year and is somewhat more than you need to solve your financial problems.

Early this morning you received a call from an individual you do not know. He indicated that he saw your advertisement and he would like to see the car.

You will meet with him shortly.

BUYER

You are a collector of antique cars. You specialize in the Rolls Royce and Bentley cars. Today you saw an advertisement in the morning paper for a 1926 Rolls Royce Silver Cloud. You have several of these cars but are always looking to add to your collection. You don't have much time available since you are here on a brief business trip. You would like to close this deal as quickly as possible. As a result, if the seller at any point asks less than *$175,000*, accept it without additional negotiation.

As you enter the garage you see the car and realize that it's in excellent shape and one you would like to buy.

Title:	THE STEREO SYSTEM	#13

Time:	Twenty Minutes

Objectives: To illustrate:

- the importance of planning and aspiration levels to negotiation success

- the variety of solutions that can lead to satisfaction

Trainer Note: This role play is very similar to Role Play #4 and should be discussed and debriefed in a similar manner.

Debriefing Note: To get maximum benefit from this negotiation, the following format is suggested.

After everyone is finished:

- Go around the room and ask people if they are satisfied. Do not allow them to say more than Yes or No.

- Then ask why they are satisfied. Most will indicate that they achieved their objective. Most will have found the planning critical.

- Ask how helpful the planning was in achieving the objective.

- Summarize responses.

- Ask people to give you their settlements. Make sure to note special issues — delivery, etc.

- After results are posted, ask for the significance of the diverse settlements. Usually there is great diversity and people will realize that there is no right answer.

- Again, look at the impact of planning on the achievement of objectives.

You are about to negotiate with a person who has been advertising a stereo system, described in the paper as "in very good condition," with "excellent sound."

The system includes the following:

- AM/FM stereo receiver with 50 watts per channel
- Record changer
- Dual cassette tape recorder
- A pair of three-way bookshelf speakers
- Wireless remote

Your brief examination of the system confirms that it is in good condition (except for some scratches on the speakers), but it does lack a CD player. Although you don't currently have any CDs, you'd like to get some in the future. Overall, the system has a good sound, but you're a little concerned about the system's lack of power (it only has 50 watts per channel).

You have $650. You have a neighbor who has a comparable system and has offered to sell it to you for $500.

You must leave for college (which is several hundred miles away) tonight, so time is critical. You would like to have the system tonight, so you could take it with you to school. You also want as much of the $650 left as possible.

Contributed by Phil Faris Associates.

You are about to negotiate with a buyer who is interested in an old stereo system you have been advertising in the paper. The buyer seemed impressed with the condition of the system (except for a few scratches on the speakers), but does not seem very enthused with its power and the fact that it doesn't have a CD player (although it does have an outlet for one).

You advertised the system for several weeks and are anxious to avoid any further advertising costs. In addition, the audio store where you are going to buy your new system has offered you $350 for it, providing you accept the offer by the end of today.

Your system has the following:

- AM/FM stereo receiver with 50 watts per channel
- Record changer
- Dual cassette tape recorder
- A pair of three-way bookshelf speakers
- Wireless remote

You would like to get as much as possible for your old system to cover the advertising expenses and to help you with the down payment on your new system.

Contributed by Phil Faris Associates.

THE SAFETY REPORTS

Time:	Thirty Minutes
Objectives:	To illustrate the need to surface underlying needs and interests.
	To practice dealing with an angry coworker.
Trainer Note:	This role play is ideal for groups that frequently deal with difficult people or where there are problems among departments.
	Ideally a brief lecture on how to deal with angry or difficult people should be conducted prior to this negotiation. The negotiation then can serve as a vehicle for practicing the model discussed in the lecture.
Debriefing Note:	In discussing this negotiation, it is helpful first to determine which groups worked out a satisfactory solution and which did not. Once this has been determined, explore what the differences were. What behaviors distinguished the successful groups from the less successful?
	Our experience has been that in those groups where this works well the parties allow each other to get their concerns out without arguing. It is important that they surface and acknowledge each others' concerns. If they begin fighting over the most recent incident and who was right, they will have a great deal of difficulty.
	If you need additional discussion information on the topic, we suggest:

> *Getting Past No* by William Ury, published by Bantam

> *Neanderthals At Work* and *Dinosaur Brains*, both by Albert Bernstein and Sydney Craft Rozen, published by Wiley

You work in Product Information. No one seems to appreciate the extent of what you do; the perception is that you take calls and fill out forms. What isn't appreciated is the number of calls that come in every day and how difficult it is to get all the necessary information from the callers, who are usually angry and annoyed and want immediate answers.

Because of the number of calls, it's not always easy to get the form completed before another call comes in. Maybe you don't always complete the form the way the folks in Product Safety would like, but sometimes you can't. You know that the fields are not always completed and your handwriting isn't perfect, but with all the pressure you're under, it's about the best you can do. In addition, you sometimes forget to let people know that someone else will also be calling them.

Jane in Safety has spoken to you about these issues several times. You've tried to explain the problem to her, but she seems to think this is something you deliberately do. You know this isn't the only thing that bothers her — Safety thinks the product complaint searches you request are just to make their life difficult. However, you have a job to do, too. There wouldn't be so many problems if all you had to do was sit and take calls, but you're always busy. You really do try to do your best when people call with problems.

You think that, more than anything else, your style drives the people in Safety crazy. On more than one occasion you've said that if you didn't make errors they'd have nothing to do. You don't think that was heard the way you meant it.

Last week you needed to take two days off. On the day you were to leave, you faxed about twenty Customer Reports to Jane. On the same day, your boss asked you to complete a report which he needed in a hurry. Just getting that done got in the way of everything else, including the forms. You were in a rush to finish the forms for Jane since you were taking off for two days. As a result, you didn't check them and there were probably more errors than normal. Rather than fixing them as she

89

usually does, Jane returned most of them (15) to you, and when you returned this morning they were sitting on your desk. She didn't need to embarrass you that way!

Your boss found out and went through the ceiling. You called Jane and are to meet with her shortly. You are furious! She needs to understand the problems you have and that everything can't be perfect. This isn't an ideal world and we all have to work together.

JANE KERR
Product Safety

You work in your firm's Product Safety Group and one of your jobs is to write up the data entry forms for customer complaints. For the most part, your work is generated by Product Information — they get the basic information from a variety of sources and send it on to you. They usually do a pretty good job, although occasionally a field will be left out, or the handwriting will be so bad that you can't figure out what is being said. Then you have to call them for clarification.

One of their people, Jack Adams, is responsible for most of the problems. Jack's forms are almost never accurately completed — it's always a safe bet that he'll leave something out. He can't even consider doing anything that might require a bit of extra effort! You need to get the complaints recorded and reported to management immediately, but his laxity frequently prevents you from doing that.

You've spoken with Jack about the problem on two separate occasions. Each time he apologizes, promises it won't happen again, and then makes some bad jokes. His standard line is, "Look, if I didn't make errors, you wouldn't have anything to do." He thinks this is funny, but you don't appreciate the humor. His work usually does get better for a few weeks, and then it's "back to normal."

Last week was the last straw! Jack faxed twenty forms to your office with a note, saying that he'd be away for several days and that "there should be no problems." You should have known better. You were too busy then to check the forms right away, and, as you expected, when you did check them all but five had at least one field missing or were incomplete. You were furious.

You talked with your boss and decided to return fifteen forms to Jack. You included a note, saying that you had been able to process only five of the original forms and that, since too much was missing, the fifteen sent back were not processed.

When Jack returned he went wild. He called in a rage, saying he was on his way to your office. You could sense how angry he was. This won't be easy but you finally got his attention!

Now that you have his attention, you want to talk with Jack about several other issues. One of them is that customers must be advised that someone will contact them for more information whenever a complaint is reported. More frequently than not, customers seem surprised when you call. In addition, you want to bring up all the individual product searches that he requests — no one else asks for as many as he does. As usual, these issues are more of a problem with Jack than with anyone else. You don't think he appreciates the problems he creates. It's almost as if he thinks you're his personal editor! You have other work to do; this constant checking back and forth with him takes too much time and is beginning to create problems for you with your boss, since you are falling behind in your own work.

You're not sure just what is going on, but it has to be settled. You need Jack's help and cooperation in order to do your job!

Title:	**THE SALARY INCREASE**	#15

Time:	Twenty Minutes

Objectives:	To practice the Six Step Model of negotiation.
	To review your firm's approach to salary issues.

Trainer Note:	This role play can be utilized to stimulate discussion about your firm's salary system and the expectations it creates for managers and supervisors. If you have recently experienced reductions in staff or a salary freeze, be careful about using this role play. It may open issues that are best left alone.

Debriefing Note:	Initially, use this role play to look at the critical skills and behaviors.
	As a follow-up, make sure to discuss the firm's salary program. This is best facilitated by looking at the different settlements and their potential impact on the employees and on the system.

Dana Vance
ENGINEERING

You have real trouble. Approximately nine months ago you hired Jack Spaulding. Jack was and is an outstanding engineer and to get him you had to offer a salary that was at the top of the range. Jack has met all of your expectations and then some. He is probably one of the two or three best people you have and you don't want to lose him. Jack usually takes on the toughest jobs, clearly enjoying the challenge and gets the job done on time and without error. When he can't get a job done he lets you know. He also has a clear list of the questions that still need to be answered so that it is clear what further steps need to be taken.

Several weeks ago, Jack came to you asking for a salary increase, pointing out that comparable salaries on the outside are much higher than he is currently getting. He mentioned several friends at companies nearby who are getting paid more than he is and who are working on assignments not nearly as complex as the ones he is asked to handle. He also pointed out that he is handling work which most of the other people can't handle and that his salary does not reflect what he is doing. Jack asked for a salary increase that would put him over the top and would make him the highest paid member of your staff.

In addition to Spaulding, two other people have come to you asking for increases, pointing to the higher salaries they could command on the outside. Neither of them are at the top of the range.

Jack asked you yesterday if you had looked into his initial request. You had to admit that you had not yet been able to, but that you would get on it immediately. He was clearly annoyed, but didn't make a big scene.

You don't want to lose Spaulding — he is the kind of employee that you need. You will shortly meet with T. Busch, the Director of Human Resources, to work out an increase for Jack and, if at all possible, for the other two.

Your department has a history of high turnover and difficulty in attracting and keeping people. You need to put a stop to this and if it means giving Jack and the others a raise, so be it!

You will meet shortly with Dana Vance of Engineering to discuss a salary problem Dana has with Jack Spaulding. Jack is a real talent, having joined the company about nine months ago. To get him, you had to approve a salary that was at the top of the range for his job. No engineer had ever been hired at that salary level, and it was not something you were comfortable doing. You approved the salary because of the pressure the engineering group was under. Turnover was high, they were working on several critical projects, and they needed Jack.

On the basis of your brief phone conversation with Dana, it appears that Jack now wants an increase. If granted, it would probably put him over the top of the range and create all sorts of problems with other employees, many of whom have been here for longer than he has.

You had a feeling this might happen when Jack was hired and warned Dana, but he insisted that Spaulding was the type of guy he needed. Now he has problems and will probably ask you to approve an increase for Jack. You have the authority to approve an increase, but you just can't do it without creating a host of other problems with other managers who all have similar problems and would love to pay their people more. The reality, however, is that this problem is going to happen again with others and won't get solved if dealt with on an individual basis.

KNOWN TO BOTH PARTIES

- Jack Spaulding is an outstanding employee.

- He has been with the firm for nine months.

- He was hired at the top of the salary range.

Title:	THE MEDICAL CONFERENCE	#16

Time:	Ten Minutes

Objectives:	To illustrate the importance of high aspirations.
	To practice Issue Identification.

Trainer Note:	This role play is best used with sales groups but is sufficiently general that it will work with any population.
	This negotiation provides an opportunity to illustrate the importance of high aspirations for both parties. Some physicians will ask for and receive the full $5,000.00. Others will ask for and receive less. Many of the sales reps will give the money away without asking for anything in return. This is very much a function of how your firm treats their "value addeds." Frequently, sales reps see the value addeds as just something available and do not see the need to ask for anything in return. They should instead see these as currencies — which you do not give away for free.

Debriefing Note:	Make sure to surface the different amounts people received. Also, ask whether the sales representative clarified exactly what the needs were before making any offers and whether he/she asked for anything in return. Frequently the reps will ask to have their company's name on the program or to participate in some way at the conference. This is very much a function of what your company usually does.
	Discuss why people received different amounts, pointing out (where you can) that those who asked for higher amounts usually received them and those reps who asked for something in return usually received it.
	At the conclusion of discussion it would be very useful to discuss your own firm's "value addeds" and how they are used. Are they just given away, or do we seek something in return? This type of discussion can be further enhanced if you have the group place a dollar amount on each of the value addeds.

TONI TEALE
Home Surgical
Sales Representative

Last week, Dr. Martin Clyde at Church Medical Center called and asked to see you. This is not something Clyde usually does. You usually have to call for appointments and frequently have to wait longer than you would like. Clyde utilizes a lot of your equipment and is generally supportive of your company.

When you asked Dr. Clyde if there was a problem, he said that he wanted to discuss your involvement in their annual conference. This is a relatively small, regional conference that Church has run for the past several years. They're probably short of money and want you to help out, but they've never asked you before.

Your company usually supports this kind of thing and it shouldn't present a problem. Your boss has pretty much given you the freedom to deal with these issues, up to a maximum of $5,000.00. You have heard that Church is attempting to get Dr. Busch to speak at the conference. Busch isn't cheap and he is probably creating a budget crunch.

You will meet with Dr. Clyde in a few minutes.

You are the Chief of Medicine at Church Medical Center. Every year you sponsor a one-day conference to update local physicians on the latest research and development. In the past you've always funded the project out of your own budget.

This is the fifth year and the conference promises to be the most successful ever. You and you staff agreed that it would be a real feather in your cap if you could get Dr. Busch to keynote the conference. Busch is one of the leading people in the field and would be a big draw. You called him last week and he is available and interested. He said that his fee for speaking is $2,500.00, plus first class airfare and hotel accommodations. You figure that the total would come to close to $5,000.00 — about twice what you usually pay. He picked up that this amount was a major shock to your system and suggested that you call the Home Surgical sales rep and have them cover his expenses. This never occurred to you; you have no idea whether they even do this sort of thing. However, you'll give it a try; you use a lot of their equipment.

You called the sales rep — something you don't usually do. When Toni asked if there was a problem, you assured her that you just wanted to talk about Home Surgical's involvement in your yearly conference. You felt uncomfortable discussing this on the phone.

Whatever support you can get will be a big help.

Title:	THE JOB POSTING	#17

Time:	Twenty Minutes
Objective:	To practice the negotiation process.
Trainer Note:	This role play can be used with any group of supervisors or managers.
	It provides a good introduction to a discussion of Equal Employment Issues, especially as they impact promotions. Your corporate EEO policy dealing with this issue should be discussed at the conclusion of this activity.
Debriefing Note:	Focus initially on the skills and behaviors that were used.
	In this role play the individual playing the Director of Field Service will frequently get very angry and annoyed when the H.R. person indicates he/she cannot do what he wants. It is interesting to explore how the H.R. person responds. Conversely, in some of the groups, this does not happen. Explore why and what happened that was different.
	As a second step explore the settlements and their impact from a morale and an EEO perspective.
	There will be groups that will argue that promoting Anita solves both the morale and EEO problems and that H.R. should be happy.
	Others will realize that we are still playing favorites and not solving the long term problem, as well as the potential problems that this creates.
	You should conclude this discussion by reviewing your company's policy on this issue.

You will meet shortly with the Director of Field Service to review a job opening that exists in the Field Service Department.

Since the director, Bill Kovacs, knows exactly who he wants to fill the job, you are sure that you will be asked to bypass the posting process.

This will not be the first time this has happened. Bill always has someone picked before a job is posted, especially if it's one that is important to him. In the past he has always been accommodated. You resent this, for it violates the job posting process which is important to the company. This type of behavior erodes people's faith in the process and creates complaints. Other managers do the same thing. Recently, two people wrote and signed a letter to the Vice President of Human Resources, claiming that the process was not fair and that they were not being given a "reasonable opportunity to bid for posted jobs." They stated that if this was to continue to be the way things were done here, they would report it to the government. The Vice President met with them and assured them he would put a stop to it. An equal employment complaint is not something you need. The company just settled a case out of court for $250,000 that involved one of your sales reps. It was a wake-up call for everyone. This is not something that is common knowledge.

The Vice President called you in and said in no uncertain terms that this was not to continue. The job posting process is an important one and critical to maintaining employee morale. He stated, "If employees perceive us as being unfair, we will have real problems. I don't want to hear about this happening again."

DIRECTOR OF
FIELD SERVICE

You will meet shortly with the Director of Human Resources about an employee you want in your department. This employee, Anita Evans, has been with the company for three months. You and she worked together at Computer Inc. and you need her in the department as quickly as possible to replace Jack Grable, who recently resigned. Anita is an excellent technician. She knows both the software and hardware and as a result is able to solve problems quickly. She would need almost no training and could pick up on Jack's work with no problem. You have already spoken with Anita and know that she is anxious to make the change and come to work for you. Anita would be the first woman promoted into this job.

You know that the folks in Human Resources will probably give you some heat for violating the posting process. But, when you emphasize the importance of this job and the skill of the employee involved, you are sure they will work something out. They always do. You don't understand why they even go through the charade of the posting process. Everyone knows that if you really want someone you can get them, and you are determined to get Anita Evans into your department. Having her would make your life so much easier. You already mentioned her to your V.P., and he agreed that she sounded like the ideal person to fill Grable's job.

Title:	THE VACATION "BUY"	#18

Time:	Twenty Minutes

Objective:	To practice the Six Step Model of negotiating.

Trainer Note:	This role play is best used with sales reps in magazine publishing.

Debriefing Note:	This negotiation requires that the sales rep make a particular effort to surface the needs and interests of the media buyer, not to focus on the client with whom he already has a relationship. If the sales rep attempts to use the client as leverage, he or she will have serious problems. This approach will frequently anger the buyer and make him or her take a much more aggressive tone. What further complicates the issue is that the buyer usually will not say what has so annoyed him/her, but just become very difficult.

You are newly appointed to the client's account and find that he is concerned about the recession. His resort business has been OK but he wants to get more bang for his buck and increase his occupancy rate. If he can get great deals, he might even consider increasing the budget, but he could cut as well for a mediocre plan. In terms of merchandising and promotions, his priorities are:

- to get people to the resort
- to get qualified leads
- to increase awareness of his new programs to the trade

His priorities in terms of position are:

- far forward
- alongside compatible edit
- ahead of competition

The client is looking for value and has indicated that he is looking to you to put together a solid package. You have many options in planning your new campaign. You are considering repeating last year's plan (3 pages each in *Modern Vacation*, *Today's "V,"* and *Vacationland*) *or* dropping one or both and adding a new book. If you take *Today's "V"* and *Vacationland*, you will have extra money to add one more page in *Modern Vacation* to keep the client happy. You have been told by the client that *Modern Vacation* is the only core book. You are considering running a larger schedule in it, but only if you can get the type of deal your client wants and deserves. He has also made it clear that you can run fewer pages in *Modern Vacation* this year. You are really anxious to impress this client and plan to work real hard at getting the right deal — you have a lot at stake personally. He has made it clear that you can divide the nine pages as you think best.

You were not involved in the planning last year, having joined the team just after the plan was approved. Last year's schedule included 3 pages in *Modern Vacation*. Merchandising included the Reader Service Page and Resort Reports, and they held a reception in their executive dining room. The client's only demand for next year is to include them. You hope he hasn't said that to their sales rep, since that would seriously limit your flexibility. What is crystal clear to you, however, is that he likes the magazine.

Modern's rep has called you several times, but you haven't met with him. This was deliberate on your part since you didn't want him to think he had a lock on the business. You have also been distant with him in your phone conversations. Let him work for the business!

You don't really read *Modern Vacation*. Your friends all like *Today's "V"* and their sales rep has met with you previously. In addition, they are offering a very attractive package.

Vacationland and *Today's "V"* have been actively pitching the business too. *Today's "V"* has proposed a huge merchandising party with a back cover ad position.

You have asked the *Modern Vacation* rep to come to a meeting to discuss what they can do.

Get your best deal! You decide which magazine you will buy and how many pages will run in each.

Be prepared to give more pages for added value.

You are a salesperson for *Modern Vacation* and have worked for them for the past two years. However, you are not new to the industry, having been in sales for a total of six years.

You are now faced with a typical situation — and one that you don't like. In several minutes you will meet with a new person from the agency representing one of your clients, a major resort. You have worked very closely with your client for the past several years, and now you have to deal with some new agency person who hardly knows you, *Modern Vacation*, or the work you've put in with the client.

Without exaggerating, you think you have a great relationship with this client. Both he and his wife read your magazine and they plan all their vacations from back issues. You have taken them both out for dinner more than once. Over the last two years you have earned your client's respect, as well as his business. He has run three pages in each of the past two years, and has been included on the Reader Service Page and Resort Reports. They also had a reception you sponsored in your executive dining room.

Unfortunately, the client has also run three pages in three other magazines. This is business you want to get. They are in planning now for next year.

The client told you that the budget for next year is less than the year before, but "not to worry, yours is the core book and will get its share of the business again next year." You want more business, not the same! You have worked hard, harder than your competitors, and you want to see an increase in business. This is an account that is important to your publisher and he would probably allow you some extra flexibility if you can significantly increase the business. If you double this business, you can make quota.

Today's "V" and *Vacationland* are your major competitors and have been trying to get more business, too. They both got three pages last year. Others have also been pitching very hard to make the list.

The client has told you confidentially that *Today's "V"* and *Vacationland* are proposing a negotiated package rate. If you know the competition, they're probably offering a good deal more.

What the client really needs are qualified leads to get people to the resort. He needs sales!

Positioning is probably important, but you are not really sure how this new person sees the world. He doesn't know the *Modern Vacation* story and you're not sure how much he knows about your relationship with the client. You've been trying to contact him, but he's not good at returning phone calls. He has, however, sent you a prepared form letter to fill out, "if you want to be included in the planning process." What an insult!

Although the client has said you will get the business, he hasn't said how much or who else will be on the list.

The agency has called you in for a meeting to "see what you can do." The goal is to negotiate an increase in the schedule. You want more than three pages.

You talked with your boss and she said to do whatever is necessary – she will work with you to sell the publisher.

Title:	**LATE AGAIN**	**#19**

Time:	Twenty Minutes
Objectives:	To practice the Six Step Model of negotiation.

To stimulate discussion on dealing with poor performance. |
| **Trainer Note:** | This negotiation should be used in a program that looks at performance problems. It will be most appropriate if your firm has a performance management program. |
| **Debriefing Note:** | This negotiation will stimulate discussion on poor performance and the supervisor's role. In looking at how they handled this role play, it is important to make sure the supervisor focused on behavior, and did not get into a discussion of the employee's "attitude" or "motivation." In addition, it is important for the supervisor to allow the employee to share his or her issues and concerns before moving into Problem Solving. |

MARIAN FORBES
Employee

You have been employed at your company for the past four months and are happy with your job. The work and people are both enjoyable. Your boss is Lee Stevens.

Lee is a low key sort of a person and only once in four months has he/she talked to you about your performance. This was about a month ago when you and several others were late returning from lunch by almost fifteen minutes. Lee didn't seem too upset and the conversation was very informal, leading you to believe that it was not too serious a problem. For the most part, Lee has not spoken to you at all about any aspect of your work. He/she just leaves you alone. This has pretty much been the case from the very beginning. He showed you the job and then you were on your own. This is the way you like to work.

Approximately two weeks ago, you were again late returning from lunch and again Lee said nothing. You guess that Lee realizes how difficult it can be to get to the cafeteria and back in forty-five minutes.

Earlier today you were late from lunch by about fifteen minutes, and Lee has just called you into the office.

LEE STEVENS
Supervisor

You are the supervisor of a small unit of seven employees. Four months ago Marian Forbes joined your department. For the initial three months Marian's work was excellent and she was never late or absent. About four weeks ago Marian was late returning from lunch by about twenty minutes. You spoke about it in a very low key sort of way, since it was only the first time it happened. She was late again last week, but because of a series of meetings you never mentioned it to her. Your own work has kept you so busy that you haven't given Marian or any of your people the attention they deserve.

Today Marian was again late returning from lunch by about 15 minutes. Your company allows 45 minutes for lunch and it can sometimes be difficult to meet the schedule, but that is the rule.

You have just asked Marian into your office to talk about this, since you want to stop the lateness before it gets any worse. Marian's work is still excellent and you don't want this to get in the way of her future.

Title:	**THE OUTBURST**	#20

Time:	Twenty Minutes
Objective:	To practice dealing with an employee incident.
Trainer Note:	This role play can be used for an entire negotiation, or solely for Issue Identification. Participants frequently rush into Problem Solving, since this incident raises sensitive issues for supervisors.
Debriefing Note:	If your company has a Labor-Management agreement or other specific policies on dealing with this type of issue, they should be discussed at the conclusion.
	In debriefing this role play it is important to explore whether the supervisor allowed the employee to discuss his/her issues and feelings. Frequently, the supervisors are so angry that they become very autocratic and do not allow the employee any room to talk. It is important that the supervisor be clear about his or her expectations, but not at the expense of allowing the employee to talk.
	If there is to be a long term solution, both parties must share their concerns before they move to Problem Solving. If you have a performance management program, you should also discuss the steps the supervisor should take after the discussion — namely, providing appropriate feedback and reinforcement as the behavior improves.

SANDY ENGLAND
Employee

Earlier today your boss asked you to finish a stack of work left over by one of your coworkers who went home sick. You were really annoyed, since you are always the person asked to fill in and complete work. Your boss never seems to ask anyone else. Every time you do this your work suffers, you fall behind, and then you have to work twice as hard to catch up. You let Dana know in no uncertain terms how annoyed you were, but you still did the work. Again, your own work has suffered and you have to work late.

Bill and Mary, both Senior Associates, recently retired and have not been replaced. This alone created even more work, without your having to cover for people who are sick. You let Dana know about your feelings this morning.

Your boss was not happy with your outburst, but you were really upset and still are. You don't know why Dana always comes to you since there are others in the department. If you're so important and so good, why don't they promote you to a Senior Associate?

Dana just called you and asked that you come to her/his office.

DANA CHAMBERS
Supervisor

Earlier today you asked one of your employees, Sandy England, to complete work that had been left undone by an employee who left early because of illness. Sandy did the work, but not before she made a scene about how she is always asked to fill in for other people. She said, "Why don't you ever ask someone else, I'm having enough trouble keeping my own work current, with Bill and Mary retired and not replaced." In addition she was loud and her complaining was heard by everyone in the department. You were very annoyed, since this should have been handled very differently by Sandy. This outburst is very out of character.

You don't understand why Sandy was so upset. The reason you turn to her is because you have so much confidence in her ability. She always completes her work, as well as any extra work that needs to be done. In fact, you and your boss have spoken on several occasions about promoting her to Senior Associate, but she will have to learn to control her temper before you do.

You have just asked her into your office to discuss what happened.

Title:	**THE POOR PERFORMANCE**	**#21**

Time:	Twenty Minutes

Objectives:	To illustrate how to deal with poor performance.
	To practice using the Six Step Model of negotiation.

Trainer Note:	As with Negotiations #19 & 20, this is ideally utilized in programs that address performance management issues.
	This is a particularly good role play for programs that include individuals who manage other managers.

Debriefing Note:	In this negotiation, people frequently confuse the issue. Rather than dealing with the performance of Rae, they focus on Rae's employee. It is important to point out that this is not the problem they should address. Only if the Issue Identification is well done is this likely to happen. If this negotiation gets off track, it is usually the people playing the manager who create the problem.

MARCIA HOFFMAN
Department Manager

You are the manager of a fairly large unit, with several supervisors who report directly to you. One of them, Rae Parker, is a relatively new supervisor who was promoted to this position from an adjacent department and who knew most of the people in your department before her appointment. One of her people, Janet Stone, has continually failed to submit her weekly status reports on time for the past six months. This is not a new problem for Janet, but it seems to have gotten progressively worse since Rae took over the department.

You have talked to Rae about the problem on two previous occasions, and each time the response is, "I talk to her but it just doesn't seem to do any good. Anyway, it's not such a serious problem, you know Janet has been having some personal problems. Besides, the work always gets done, so what's the big deal?" Rae never fails to assure you that a talk will be held with Janet soon. Needless to say, the problem has not improved and you have just called Rae into your office to discuss the matter again, before it begins to spread and creates more serious production problems.

Known to Both Parties

Rae has been a supervisor for two months.

RAE PARKER
Supervisor

You were recently appointed supervisor in the department managed by Marcia Hoffman.

Ever since you were appointed, Marcia has been on you about Janet Stone — having talked to you on several occasions about her. You have spoken with Janet. Her work improves for a while, and then slips back. Janet is late with her reports and always has been. So why is Marcia making such a big issue of it now? Anyway, Janet's other work is as good, if not better, than anyone's in the unit. When it comes to customer contact, no one is better. She is dependable and can handle the most difficult problems. Besides, you know that Janet is having family problems. You have mentioned them to Marcia each time the issue of Janet Stone is raised. These are problems, which if left alone, will probably solve themselves and so will Janet's work. Janet has been with the company for many years. She knows what she is supposed to do.

You are a new supervisor and they cannot expect you to undo all the problems created by the people who preceded you. Your goal is to take care of the most important problems first, and this surely is not one of them.

Known to Both Parties

Rae has been a supervisor for two months.

Title:	**THE DISTRICT MANAGER**	#22

Time:	Twenty Minutes

Objectives:	To practice the Successful Negotiator model.
	To discuss issues unique to remote management — especially as it affects sales force management.

Trainer Note:	This role play should be used as part of a sales management program.
	Sales managers face this problem with their reps as well as with their Regional Managers, as outlined in this role play.

Debriefing Note:	The Regional Managers that handle this well, do several things correctly. Namely, they do Issue Identification, allow the employee to share their concerns, are clear about their expectations, and are open to working with the employee to solve the problem.
	This role play will provide a springboard for a discussion of remote management issues. If you are working with a group of District or Sales Managers, use this negotiation to explore both how this issue affects them, and how they deal with the problem. We have found it helpful to do a problem census and then to have the group do some group problem solving around individual situations.

J.T.
Regional Director

You are a Regional Director with four District Managers reporting directly to you. Three of them have been in their jobs for several years; you are generally pleased with all three. This other DM, Jim Baker, is new and has been in his position for only six months. Like most DMs, he was an outstanding sales rep before being promoted. Jim came from another region into this job.

Jim has not yet made the transition from sales rep to effective manager. He spends far too much time traveling with his reps, which means that he's not in his office when other reps have problems or when you need to talk to him. You have spoken with him about this several times, and, while he says he understands, his behavior changes only for a short period. Soon, he's back on the road with his reps again.

The problem has come to a head recently. Twice last week it took him a day to return your call and to address issues you had raised with him. To make matters worse, his comments on the national sales conference were not sent in on time, indicating that he is not spending adequate time in the office or making the best use of his time. More serious was that his input was needed immediately, so that the planning could be completed.

Jim's behavior can't continue. Since he is at the home office today, you asked him to meet with you later to discuss his performance. You really need to get this straightened out, since Jim has a great deal of potential and you don't want to see it wasted.

JIM BAKER
District Manager

You are a recently appointed District Manager, having been promoted six months ago. So far at least, you have enjoyed your job. The other District Managers in your region have been in their jobs for several years and all have good solid reputations.

Since you came to your new position from another region, the sales reps who report to you are all new. As a result, you have been on the road with them as much as possible. This has given you the opportunity to get to know them and, where necessary, to help them and allow them to know you. This is the way your DM worked with you and you really appreciated it.

However, your current boss, J.T., is not happy with your "time management skills" as she calls them. J.T. has spoken with you twice about the need to balance your time between travel and office and to fulfill your management responsibilities. You try to comply as much as possible, but it doesn't seem right to you. You need to be in the field doing what you do best — working with reps. The paperwork always gets done — even if it is a bit late.

J.T. tried to reach you twice last week and got really upset when you were slow to respond. You got back to her the next morning, but she wasn't happy. She also was upset because you didn't get some paperwork for the national sales conference into the home office on time, causing a fair amount of confusion. To make things worse, this isn't the first time that you've been late with reports. You never realized just how critical paperwork was — it's a real pain.

J.T. has asked to meet with you later today since you are in the home office. You are not looking forward to this meeting.

Title:	**THE SOFTWARE SYSTEM**	**#23**

Time:	Thirty Minutes

Objective:	To practice the Six Step Model of negotiation.

Trainer Note:	This is a negotiation that should be used to illustrate issues presented when coworkers negotiate.

Debriefing Note:	It is particularly important that both the issues and the underlying needs and interests of both parties be brought to the surface in this negotiation. In the early stages it is important that both sides listen to and acknowledge each other's concerns. Very frequently, they will begin to argue over the time and not get beyond that issue. If they identify all the issues, and not diminish each others' concerns, their ability to solve the problem will be greatly enhanced. There needs to be an atmosphere that says, "We can share our fears and concerns with each other and then find a reasonable solution."

You are Matt Jones, the Director of Systems Development. You have been with your company for about four years. You really enjoy your day-to-day work, but don't like the number of meetings you have to sit through or the different personalities you have to put up with.

Just yesterday you found that you had been appointed as the manager on a new project — one that Systems Planning wants to implement as soon as possible. It seems that they want to add new information to the Financial Reporting System. This project was started last year, but was put aside because of more pressing matters. You should have known that something was afoot when last week Sally Bass called you and asked, "Just hypothetically, Matt, how long do you think it would take to fix the Reporting system?" As usual, you tried to avoid giving an answer, but she was very persistent and got you to commit yourself to six months. You hate when people do that. Why not just be up front and honest about what you need?

You and several others spent most of last week putting together an initial proposal, taking into account all the specs described by Sally last year. You all agreed that if this job was put off last year, it couldn't be that urgent now. However, Sally's people think that everything is urgent. In addition, they expect you to give them what they want when they want it — and in the past, you've always delivered for them.

Sally asked you for a formal proposal. You spelled out everything as clearly as you could and stated that the time to execute this project will be, at a minimum, eight months. When you gave Sally that six month time estimate several weeks ago, it turned out to be too short, especially in the face of your staffing situation. Your people have been working practically night and day for several months now and are spread very thin. In fact, several important mistakes were picked up during the past months on one project — one on which your staff was working very hard. So hard, in fact, that you think the errors were due to their fatigue. So, although you think you could pull this new job off in six months, you don't want to push your people — you don't want any more errors!

145

In addition, you're worried about QA's ability to give you the people to check out the software. If everything goes smoothly, you should be able to make the eight month projection with no trouble. To do any better would require assistance from Sally. Your boss said, "Do whatever you need to get this thing completed. It's your department. You know your people and what needs to get done."

Sally called you this morning and asked to meet with you to discuss "certain elements of your proposal." You wonder what she's up to now.

You are the Director of Systems Planning. You were promoted into this position about three years ago and have been taking on more and more assignments with increasing responsibilities. Your boss has asked you to work on a new project — one which will add new information into the Financial Reporting System. This same project began last year, but another, very urgent situation arose and work on this one was put on hold. Everyone now feels that this project can't wait and should be done even faster because of last year's delay. This is particularly important to your boss; last year he had serious problems when Corporate asked for a detailed analysis of overseas transactions and we did not have the data readily available.

This is the first project you have ever headed and you want it to go well. Even more importantly, your boss *needs* it accomplished quickly and efficiently. Several weeks ago he asked you to research how long the enhancements on the system would take to get up and running. He needed the information to prepare for a planning meeting.

In an effort to get this information, you made an informal call to Matt Jones, the Director of Systems Development, whom you know fairly well. Making it sound real casual (you hoped), you asked him — hypothetically — for a ballpark figure on the time it would take to rework the system.

At first, Matt reacted very strongly and insisted that he couldn't possibly give you an answer. He said it would be "way off, more of an 'out in left field' response than a ballpark figure." You persisted, assuring him that it didn't matter — just as long as it was somewhere close. After a bit, Matt gave in and told you it would most likely take about 6 months. You thanked him and gave this information to your boss. Matt was probably exaggerating the time by at least one month, probably two, to protect himself.

In turn, your boss invited you to his senior staff meeting, where he announced that you would take the lead on this project. Although your boss related the six month completion figure, everyone there said it was much too long. They asked to have the project completed in four months

— at most five. Everyone agreed that Systems Development always tacked on a little excess time to every project. They're known as being superconservative, insisting on testing every system for longer than necessary. They tend to exaggerate the complexity and how hard it is to make changes. However, they always seem to meet the schedules.

Shortly after the meeting, you made a phone call to Matt to request a formal proposal to revamp the financial reporting system based on last year's specifications. He advised you that one would be on your desk in about a week.

Within a week, as you expected, you received the proposal. As you suspected, the time estimate was far too long. Matt is now proposing eight months — which is two months longer than his original estimate. We need this handled very aggressively — if they're involved in other projects, they should put them aside. You have some extra money in your budget and would be willing to hire some outside consultants to help them out, if necessary. In essence, your boss told you to do whatever you need to get this project done. He said, "You have my full confidence — and support."

You have your first meeting today with Matt. That meeting will be held in fifteen minutes.

Title:	**SUPERMARKET BUYER**	**#24**

Time:	Twenty Minutes

Objectives:	To practice the Six Step Model of negotiation.
	To practice Issue Identification.

Trainer Note:	This particular role play will work only with supermarket groups and should not be used with other participants unless you make significant changes. The Buyer's role-play talks about getting the "right deal." We have not defined that term — but leave it to each participant to define in the context of your company.

Debriefing Note:	In debriefing this role play, pay particular attention to how well the vendor did Issue Identification and its impact on overall satisfaction and quality of the deal. The vendor has a lot to work with. Frequently they will not do a very effective job at Issue Identification, but will assume they understand the buyer's concerns and will begin making offers. The buyer, in turn, ends up with a good deal and is happy, but the vendor has given away more than necessary.

BETTY MORRIS
Buyer — Grocery

You have been a Super X buyer in grocery for the past two and one-half years, having worked your way up from a shipping clerk when you were first hired seven years ago. You know the business, inside and out, and you've learned it the hard way.

You have a reputation for being tough with vendors and you like it that way. If vendors think you're weak, they'll try to sell you whatever they can at whatever price they can get — just to up their commission.

You have a vendor coming in shortly from a company which is new to this area. The guy sounded good over the phone, but then, they all try to sound good. You decided to give him an appointment after you saw one of his products displayed in an A&P in Denver this summer when you were on vacation. It was a nonalcoholic, imported beer with less calories than the other brands. You tried it and it tastes terrific. The packaging is good — foil wrapped and an unusually shaped bottle.

You need another line in this area — something which will attract customers to the beer area. Sales have been down for the past two months, even during the normally heavy summer months, and you can't let them stay there.

Maybe if you take on a low calorie youth-oriented product, it will bring life back into the whole section. The Lite Beers took off for a while, but your feeling is that they appealed to the older, weight-conscious population. You think this line will sell to the young, health conscious, Evian crowd.

If you can get a good opening deal, one that will allow Super V to break the product in this area, along with a healthy advertising and slotting allowance, you may be able to convince Sam, your boss, to try it. Sam doesn't like to take risks, especially with new companies. He's told you that he'll consider this product if you can get the right deal. You have a real feeling about this item and, even though you'd be taking a risk on it, you think it's what your area needs to pull it out of its slump. Yet, you're somewhat hesitant to begin business with a new untried company and one that is based in the Midwest where shipping and delivery will be problems.

You will meet with the vendor shortly.

Known to Both Parties

Cantwell has a new nonalcoholic beer that they wish to introduce into the Northeast market.

Cantwell is new to the Northeast. They have done well with their product in the Midwest and the West.

You are a salesman for Cantwell, a food company based in the Midwest. The company has done well in the West and Midwest and is just now expanding into the Northeast. You've worked as a sales rep for several major food companies during your twelve-year career, but never with beverages, and you're just beginning to appreciate some of the problems involved. Now Cantwell has a new line of nonalcoholic beers which has taken off in the West. You're sure that it'll do as well in the Northeast and are looking for the right chain to break it.

You've gotten yourself an appointment with the Super X beverage buyer and will meet with her shortly. You're not sure that Super V has the right customer profile for your product, since it's higher priced than the national brands, but this pricing policy has worked well in other areas to attract the "young professional." You have a fairly generous advertising allowance and opening program to work with. You've been told by your management to do whatever is necessary to establish this product in one or two supermarket chains in this territory.

You're about to meet with the buyer; you're sure that one of her issues will be shipping and delivery schedules, since your bottling plants are in the Midwest, but you're prepared to deal with that one. Your company will be establishing warehouse facilities around the country.

You have ten minutes to plan for this meeting.

Known to Both Parties

Cantwell has a new nonalcoholic beer that they wish to introduce into the Northeast market.

Cantwell is new to the Northeast. They have done well with their product in the Midwest and the West.

Title:	**THE HABA BUYER**	#25

Time:	Twenty Minutes

Objectives:	To practice the Six Step Model of negotiation.
	To explore issues unique to supermarket buying.

Trainer Note:	As with Role Play #24, the role play should only be used with supermarket buyers or people who sell to them. The two negotiations work well together.

Debriefing:	As with the previous negotiation, pay particular attention to how well the vendor completes Issue Identification. They tend not to do this well, but move very quickly to making offers. Explore the implications of doing this. Also lead a discussion on how the Issue Identification should have been done.

You are a sales representative for Health Systems, a small company which makes Dento, a toothpaste which rids the teeth of plaque. The toothpaste is the only one on the market which accomplishes this, and it's now being recommended by oral hygienists. Sometimes you wish that your company was one of the giants, so that you could do a huge marketing campaign on the product — then it would really take off.

Today you are going to meet with Sam Shepherd, Garys' HABA products buyer. You told Sam that you're going to make a preliminary presentation on a new product, soon to be released by your firm. This new product is another toothpaste, and, in addition to its cavity and plaque fighting features, will also rid the mouth of up to 60% of tartar. Like Dento, it will be 50% more expensive than the brand names, but for this new product, Health Systems is doing a radio and print campaign. There will even be a spot on Good Morning America, in which the company president will discuss its benefits.

You are prepared to make Gary an opening deal which will include the right to break the product in all their areas, a 10% discount for a three-month period, a slotting allowance, and an advertising allowance of $35,000 over a six-month period.

If necessary, you've been authorized to throw in a coupon drop, to be coordinated with Garys' January Sale.

Known to Both Parties

- Health Systems and Garys have been doing business for several years.

- The relationship between Sam and Harriet is a good one.

- Health Systems now makes a specialized toothpaste — Dento.

- Dento is both effective and expensive.

- Health Systems has not marketed heavily.

You are a buyer in Garys' Health and Beauty aids. You have been a buyer for two years, having been promoted from buyer trainee in the same department. You are now responsible for buying all oral hygiene products, and although you like HABA, the number of products is maddening. No sooner does one company come out with a new polka dotted toothpaste, then every other manufacturer has a me-too, polka dotted toothpaste. You simply don't have room, either in the warehouse or the stores, for so many varieties. Yet, the customer wants whatever is advertised.

As you look at your watch, you realize that you have an appointment in a few minutes with Harriet Slade, a salesperson for Health Systems. You've worked with Harriet for several years and like her a lot. When Harriet set up the appointment, she mentioned that Health Systems has a new product she wants to show you — you pray that it isn't another toothpaste! Health Systems now makes Dento, a specialized toothpaste that reduces plaque. Although the toothpaste works (you use it yourself), it doesn't have a large market, probably because it is so expensive, but also because the company doesn't market heavily. But you still feel that you should carry Dento for those customers who want it.

Known to Both Parties

- Health Systems and Garys have been doing business for several years.

- The relationship between Sam and Harriet is a good one.

- Health Systems now makes a specialized toothpaste — Dento.

- Dento is both effective and expensive.

- Health Systems has not marketed heavily.

Support Materials

Introduction

This section contains materials that you will find helpful in conducting the practice negotiations. Included are Planning Forms, an Observer Sheet, and a Debriefing worksheet.

Skill Identification Sheet

This is a worksheet that participants complete prior to the negotiation to help them focus on the skills they need to practice. In addition, if observers are being used, we have them share the sheet with their observer. This allows the observer to pay particular attention to behaviors that are important to the individual doing the role play.

Planning Forms

These forms should be used for the planning process. Depending on the complexity of the negotiation, we suggest that you allow between fifteen and thirty minutes. If the group is large enough, have people work with another person. After the negotiation, talk about the value and importance of the planning. People should be encouraged to keep the planning sheets with them during the negotiation.

Observer Sheet

Each person should have an observer, if possible. We suggest that the negotiator meet with their observer to identify what behaviors they want to practice. On the second sheet there are several negative behaviors. They are there only because people use them and it is important to explore their implications. In addition, there are several blank spaces where people can add any behaviors that are not listed and that they may want to practice.

Debriefing Sheet

These sheets are designed to help participants identify what they did well and what they did poorly — in short, to assess how they did. If you are utilizing observers, have them distribute the debriefing sheets. The observers should lead the debriefing discussions in small groups.

If observers are not being used, give out the debriefing sheets to the negotiators as the groups finish. Each negotiator should complete a worksheet and then, using the debriefing sheets, discuss and review how they did.

Critical Behaviors

This is a description of the behaviors we think are most important for the Successful Negotiator. At the conclusion is a grid, which shows the steps in the process and the behaviors critical to each step.

Practice Negotiating Directions

This is a handout that gives the negotiator general directions on how to "role play." While helpful to all negotiators, it is especially beneficial for the individuals who previously have not done role playing.

SKILL IDENTIFICATION

Directions

I want to practice the following skills in the upcoming negotiation.

_____

_____

_____

_____

_____

_____

_____

_____

_____

_____

_____

_____

_____

_____

_____

Directions

1) What are your objectives for the upcoming negotiation? Be as specific as possible. What are your –

   HOPE to gets — Nice to have

   INTEND to gets — Important

   MUST gets — Possible deal breaker

2) What do you think are the other party's –

   HOPE to gets

   INTEND to gets

   MUST gets

3) What do you think they need so they can say yes to you?

4) What questions do you need to ask?

5) What questions do you think they will ask you?

Planning Worksheet Summary

	ME	OTHER PARTY
ISSUES (Why we are meeting)		
OBJECTIVES (What is wanted)		
PERCEIVED NEEDS AND INTERESTS (Feelings)		
POTENTIAL CONCESSIONS (Things I'm willing to give up)		
SETTLEMENT OPTIONS (Possible solutions to the issues)		

THE SUCCESSFUL NEGOTIATOR

OBSERVER WOOKSHEET

Selected Behaviors

BEHAVIOR	Climate Setting		Issue Identification		Bargaining		Settlement	
Asked questions								
Clarified – positions – needs and interests								
Summarized – during the negotiation – at the conclusion								
Checked for understanding								
Actively listened								
Made contingent concessions								
Shared needs and interests								
Proposed solutions								
Established common ground								
Solicited solutions								
Focused on the problem								

THE SUCCESSFUL NEGOTIATOR

OBSERVER WOOKSHEET

Selected Behaviors

BEHAVIOR	Climate Setting		Issue Identification		Bargaining		Settlement	
Acknowledged efforts								
Expanded the pie								
Listened actively								
Made judgments or threats								
Fixed blame								
Used a patronizing or generally hostile tone								
Interrupted								

1) How satisfied are you with your performance?

Very Satisfied   → → → → → → → → → → →   Very Dissatisfied
      5   4   3   2   1

Please explain:

2) What do you feel most satisfied about?

3) How well did you practice your "critical behaviors"?

4) What would you like to have done differently?

CRITICAL BEHAVIORS

Introduction

We believe these behaviors are critical to implementing the Successful Negotiator model. We have identified the behaviors through our own experience and observation, as well as a review of the literature on negotiation. If you use our model and observer sheets, we urge that you use this material as the basis of a lecture prior to the initiation of any role plays.

Questioning

Negotiators are always asking a variety of questions — from open-ended, information seeking to more closed-ended, lightly focused questions. Good negotiators utilize questioning to gather information.

Clarifying

To ensure mutual understanding of what has been said before moving to the next topic.

Checking for Understanding

Where Clarifying looks at what is being said, Checking for Understanding looks at the feelings that people may be experiencing, but not sharing.

Summarizing

This behavior brings together several ideas that are being discussed or that have been agreed to by the parties. This behavior ensures that there is no misunderstanding. Summarizing should be utilized continuously through-out the negotiation. When done during the negotiation, it serves to reinforce that the negotiators are making progress and will reach a solution.

Active Listening

This behavior is best demonstrated by lack of interruptions and ensures that both parties are able to say what they want. It is also critical to bringing the underlying needs and interests to the table.

Sharing Needs and Interests

This behavior is very much a result of the previous behaviors. A climate of openness and trust is established which allows people to share their needs and interests. Getting the needs and interests on the table allows for more creativity in finding a solution.

Focusing on the Problem

To be successful during the Issue Identification and Bargaining stage, it is important to stay focused on the problem and to limit the amount of verbal wandering. Staying focused is also helped through the use of clarifying and summarizing.

Seeking Solutions

In this behavior we ask the other party what he/she sees as the answer or possible solution. When seeking solutions, it is important to clarify the nature of the proposal before responding. Too frequently people just respond with a "yes" or a "no." Unless there is a high degree of trust, this behavior and the two that follow should not be utilized before Bargaining.

Proposing Solutions

The exact opposite of the previous behavior, in that here we offer our own ideas as to the possible solution.

Contingent Concessions

When they make concessions, most people just give things away and hope that the other person will somehow respond in kind. Contingent concessions are those where you identify the *quid pro quo* when you make a concession. Basically, what is it that you want in return for your concession?

Acknowledging Efforts

This is a fancy term for providing reinforcement for what the other person does or says during the negotiation, i.e., "That's a good point."

Expanding the Pie

This is a critical problem solving behavior that helps the parties look beyond the obvious. Frequently, parties offer a "compromise" or "split the difference," and when this happens, neither party is very happy because the focus is usually on the positions. To expand the pie, one must incorporate the underlying needs and interests to find a solution, not just focus on positions.

Establishing Common Ground

Very effective in climate setting, it provides a bond between the parties, and establishes them as people working toward a solution.

Prior Experience

This is primarily a climate setting behavior where the parties discuss positive prior experiences. They might also discuss a prior negative experience, in a way which helps them to learn from it.

This list is not meant to include all of the behavior negotiators are to use, but to serve as a beginning. Feel free to add to this list.

ROLE PLAYING / PRACTICE NEGOTIATING

Directions

Role playing affords the opportunity to try out new behaviors in a supportive setting, but many people become anxious when asked to role play. To make role playing work for you and to aid the learning process, we suggest the following:

- There are no correct answers and as such, there is no script that you must follow.

- Accept the facts of the situation as they are written.

- You should assume whatever "attitude" is described ... however, once the role play begins, you can allow your feelings to take over.

- If issues arise that are not covered in the role you were assigned, feel free to add facts. The facts, however, should be consistent with how the situation could play out.

- Don't say, "this isn't how it would happen in real life." For the purposes of this exercise, this *is* real life.

- Don't try to be an actor ... that's not the objective. To the degree possible, be yourself.

- HAVE FUN!